Table of Content

NIU Publishing. February 2016

Preface

I wrote this book to give many students and professionals an understanding of lean enterprise in any of its form such as lean manufacturing, lean services, or lean product development. It is the first module of four modules. Working for manufacturing businesses, I found that lean enterprise was often misunderstood. Many books also miss an emphasis on the foundations of lean enterprise which are the lean principles and the understanding of waste.

I have enunciated three different sets of lean principles. The three sets of principles are equivalent but the fourteen Toyota's principles are more detailed. Jeffrey Liker took the time to break down the principles enunciated by Taiichi Ohno, Seichi Nakajima, Shigeo Shingo, and the earlier Toyota senior executives into manageable principles, more functionally focused for a better understanding. For that reason, I gave many examples that clarify the fourteen principles. I did not intend to cheer Toyota but although the ideas of waste elimination and respect for people started at Ford Motor Company with Henry Ford, the works done by Taiichi Ohno, Seichi Nakajima, Shigeo Shingo, and the earlier Toyota senior executives have paved the way to the management framework we called today lean enterprise. I have been quite detailed on wastes.

It makes a huge difference in the management of operations when employees and managers understand what waste is, and when they understand wastes that are necessary versus wastes that are unnecessary. I have broken down wastes from quality defects and rework into two groups: wastes driven by manufacturing or services and wastes driven by design. I have broken down wastes from poor utilization of resources into two groups: wastes from poor utilization of human capital and wastes from poor utilization of non human capital resources. Wastes from poor utilization of human capital include poor utilization of people in their work and poor utilization of people intellectual assets such as patents and tacit knowledge. I have also introduced a new waste which is the waste driven by non compliance to organizational code of conduct which includes (but is not limited to) ethical principles and the laws. Managers and workers in general need to eliminate all the nine wastes described in this book otherwise their business may never maximize its full potential.

Finally, I have tried to make the book easy to read. The examples and exercises address dilemmas that managers often face in today's businesses. The cases, exercises, and problems may be challenging because I selected them to suit a senior undergraduate audience, MBA programs, and Executive MBA programs. For many exercises students ought to solve problems or ask questions related to their job, enabling them to immediately apply the learning. I will be available to welcome feedback at gregoiren@yahoo.com

Regards,

Gregoire Nleme.

Chapter One
Introduction to Lean Enterprise

1.1) Purpose of this Book and Definitions of Lean Enterprise

This book is for anyone who wants to learn about and apply lean enterprise. It provides a solid foundation made of several examples, exercises, problems, and cases that if followed with discipline should help the learner make a difference in her or his organization. Specialists, supervisors, managers, executives, and instructors should benefit from this Module 1 manual.

1.1.1) Outcomes from reading this book
Readers will be able to define lean enterprise and will know lean principles as described by different experts

Readers will know the difference between value adding and non value adding activities in manufacturing or in services

Readers will be able to quickly identify value adding activities that are necessary or not necessary and non value adding activities that are necessary or not necessary

Readers will know the different types of waste in current for profits or not for profit organizations, more, they will probably discover new types of waste.

Readers will be able to understand and identify unnecessary waste, and take the next steps to eliminate it.

Readers will be better prepared for further development in lean manufacturing or lean product development.

1.1.2) Definition of lean manufacturing
Lean Manufacturing is a manufacturing system that is committed to and follows these principles (Ohno, 1988; Womack, 1990)

Empowering employees to make decisions

Fostering Management to be coaches instead of bosses

Elimination of waste within the whole value stream

Living as a learning organization where mistakes are accepted as improvement opportunities and where knowledge is a capability

Managers making decisions with long terms considerations on the business and on the community

1.1.3) Definition 1 of a Lean Enterprise (Henderson & Larco, 1999; Kennedy, 2003; Ohno, 1988; Shingo, 1985; Womack et al., 1992)
Lean Enterprise is a business system where management and all employees are committed to and follow these principles

1. Long term strategy, meaning adaptive strategic intent
2. Managers as coaches, leaders at all levels
3. Voice of the Customer, which implies use of a pull system
4. Minimization of waste

5. Robust control and prevention of problems - learning from the past and taking the time to fix
6. Continuous improvement – evolving standardized processes and continuous learning
7. Collaboration with your stakeholders
8. Respect for and development of your employees (technical and business maturity.

The definition of lean manufacturing is equivalent to the one I just listed above with eight principles for manufacturing enterprises but the definition with eight principles is more detailed. Definition 1 of lean enterprise that I just described with eight principles is equivalent to definition 2 because the eight principles just described are equivalent to the Toyota Way's fourteen principles enunciated by Jeffrey Liker of the University of Michigan (next page). The Toyota Way's principles are more detailed. For instance the Toyota Way principles 6, 12, 13, and 14 clarify continuous improvement (principle 6 above). Toyota Way principles 2, 5, 7, 8, 12, and 13 clarify how employees should stop to solve problem (principles 4 and 5 above). Toyota Way Principles 9, 10, 11 clarify the development of employees. Seemingly, a manufacturing organization that follows the eight principles just described or the fourteen principles of the Toyota way is a lean manufacturing organization. Toyota's leaders and experts with a great mention to Taiichi Ohno and Shigeo Shingo developed the tools and principles that constitute the management framework known today as lean manufacturing. I will list the Toyota way principles proposed by Jeffrey Liker of the University of Michigan and will clarify the meaning of each of the principles in italic

1.1.4) Definition 2 of a Lean Enterprise
A lean enterprise is an enterprise that follows the fourteen's Toyota way principles:
1. Make decision for the long term
2. Continuous process flow
3. Use a pull system
4. Level out the workload (Heijunka)
5. Stop to fix problem (Jidoka)
6. Standardized tasks are the foundation for continuous improvement
7. Use visual management and control to avoid hiding concerns
8. Make sure that you use technology that are reliable and have been proven robust.
9. Develop leaders who thoroughly understand your business
10. Develop outstanding people and teams
11. Respect your partners
12. Go see where the problem occurs so you can better understand
13. Take time and use consensus to make decisions
14. Grow to become a learning organization

Definition 1 and definition 2 are equivalent because the two set of principles are equivalent but I will use definition 2 from this point to the last page of the book because it is more detailed.

4

I.2) A Brief History of Lean Enterprise

All started with Taylor's scientific management and the Henry Ford's assembly line and waste reduction model of 1903-1939. Henry Ford thought that his company needed to treat its employees well for two main reasons. First if the company treated them well then Ford Motor Company's employees would be motivated to come to work and do a good job. Second by paying its employees well, Henry Ford was creating a middle class that could purchase Ford vehicles while developing the community for a larger middle class.

Toyota's executives visited Ford Motor Company plant between 1935 and 1939 and went back to Japan and started implementing the concepts just described above. Toyota had just been incorporated as an automobile manufacturer in 1937 and it is fair to say that Toyota started implementing lean enterprise at its birth. Toyota executive refined lean processes through continuous learning with adjustments. From the 1950s to the 1970s, Taiichi Ohno, Shiego Shingo and Seichi Nakajima refined many lean concepts such as just-time, Kanban, Jidoka, total productive maintenance (TPM), and single minute exchange of dies (SMED), without any doubt the Toyota Production System had become mature with results translated into increases in worldwide market shares of automobiles.

Toyota had entered the USA market at the end of the 1950s and in those days as a new entrant its vehicles had little brand value in the USA market. From 1975 to 1989, sales of Toyota vehicles in the USA were steadily growing while sales of the Big Three cars were decreasing. Toyota had become a significant player in the USA market. In1990, James Womack wrote the best seller "the machine that changed the word" and used the term "Lean Manufacturing" while describing TPS. The name became commonly accepted in the U.S. and is now accepted worldwide as a synonym of a management philosophy that embraces a systemic view of the business and that complies with the lean principles that I just described in the first few pages of this book.

1.3) Exercises 1

Exercises 1.1
Q1.1) What are the benefits of empowering employees ?
Q1.2) Give examples of employees who are empowered to make decision
Q1.3) can a business empower employees who are not very good employees?

Exercises 1.2
Q2.1) What are the consequences of managers being bosses more than coaches?
Q2.2) What are the consequences of managers being coaches more than bosses?

Exercises 1.3
Q3.1) Write a short essay (one page to two pages) to explain with examples "mistakes are accepted as opportunities of improvement"
Q3.2) Write a short essay with examples to explain why knowledge is a capability

Chapter 2
The Fourteen Toyota Way's Lean Principles per Jeffrey Liker
(Liker, 2004)

Business professionals also call these principles the Toyota Way principles. I will list each principle and provides some explanation for clarification. I will also sometime provide illustrative examples. An organization that follows the 14 principles is a lean enterprise.

2.1) Make decision for the long term (Ohno, 1988)

A business needs to have a strategic intent and a mission that gives its employees a meaning beyond just making products. Toyota was relatively a late entrant in the first half of the 20th century (incorporated in 1937). Some extracts of Toyota's missions:

2.1.1) Making thing is important and

2.1.2) We try to help people and society

Not making decision for the long term may drive a business out of its strategic intent. When managers make decisions for the short terms they introduce unintended consequences that hurt the business in a long run. For instance a company may downsize too early because of quarterly indicators of market decline, parting away with creative employees that it may need just a few months after the market picks up.

2.2) Continuous process flow

When the process is standardized and stabilized, it creates high value with quality and reliable products cycle after cycle. This is not just valid for manufacturing but it is also valid for product development and services. Continuous one piece flow is a characteristic needed for assembly operations. One piece flow allows managers and other workers to focus on the attributes of one product at a time. One piece flow also leads to a shorter lead time when compared to the flow of batches of parts, thus better quality since defects are not spread to the many products of a batch. If an operator or a group of operators have to work on five products at the time, it becomes more difficult to find out which product left the workstation with defects.

Table 1
One Piece Flow Assembly Line versus Batch Assembly Line

One Piece Flow Fine			
Workstation 1	**Workstation 2**	**Workstation 3**	**Workstation 4**
A_1	B_1	C_1	D_1
Bach Line			
Workstation 1	**Workstation 2**	**Workstation 3**	**Workstation 4**
$A_1B_1C_1D_1$	$A_2B_2C_2D_2$	$A_3B_3C_3D_3$	$A_4B_4C_4D_4$

In the example that I am displaying on Table 1, it takes an operator one minute to work on each product A_i, B_i, C_i, and D_i. If the probability for having a defect out of one product is 1 out of 1000 or 0.0001 then the probability of have a defect out of one workstation in the case of batch system is 4 out of 10000 or 0.0004 or 400% more chance to have a defect out of a workstation in a batch line than in a one piece flow line. Besides since the cycle time for each product in a one piece flow line is one minute, the lead time for each product, from workstation 1 to workstation 4 will be four minutes in the one piece flow line but it will be 16 minutes in a the batch line. One piece flow help shorten the manufacturing lead time.

Here below are other implications of this principle.

Since continuous flow is the ideal, then areas or instances of non continuous flows should be areas of great attention. These are areas where they are many opportunities for variations and for improvement. In manufacturing, examples are instances when the line is down, a process team just installed new equipment, a manager hired a new workforce, or a cross-functional team is launching a new product. In product development; a relevant example is an instance of an engineering change, a start of a new program, or a build of new prototypes. For process manufacturing such as heat treatment or industrial bakeries (for instance a Sara Lee's bread plant in the USA), an instance of batch changes is a relevant example.

2.3) Use a pull system

Managers should scale their resources and their production to the customers' wants (volume and attributes) otherwise there will be rebates, discounts, sales, thus lower perceived brand equity. In the automobile industry, over-capacity is usually a long term consequence of a marginal use or a poor use of a pull system. The opposite of a pull system is a push system. In a push system managers make their workforce produce too many products while expecting to have enough customers to purchase all the quantities of finished products available. In a competitive market a push system leads to inventories of finished products. To sell the inventories of products, managers issue rebates and other incentives that drive profit margins and brand equity down.

2.4) Level out the workload or the schedule (Heijunka in Japanese)

Here are a few illustrations of this principle:

When balancing an assembly line, the objective is to have all the workstations equally busy to minimize waste. The ideal production time for each workstation should be equal to the tack time or as close as possible to the tack time (exact production time divided by demand in a given period) otherwise some operators will be idle when others will be busy working

Homogeneity in the production schedule is another example. Let us consider the demand of a product of feature X, Y, and Z as 40000X, 50000Y, and 10000Z at a production rate of 200 units per hour, a planning supervisor must level out the schedule by setting up this flow of work-in-process: 80X, 100Y, and 20Z every hour rather than this flow: first all the X for 200 hours, all the Y for 250 hours, and all the Z for 50 hours.

2.5) Stop to fix problems – autonomation (Jidoka)

The use of an Andon system is an illustration. An Andon system is a system of display boards that alerts workers of a potential quality or equipment downtime somewhere in the assembly line or in the work cell. Autonomation means automation led by human beings. Jidoka means the line may stop automatically if there is a quality problem. Jidoka is synonym of an automated mistake proofing device. Poka Yoke means mistake proofing device in Japanese. There are also Poka Yoke devices that are not automated but mechanical. For quality characteristics that do not have Poka Yoke, it is necessary for process experts to include an inspection loop in the workstation so the operator can stop the line if he or she forgets or makes a mistake on a characteristic.

Here is an example. A production line is making 50 products per hour on a ten hour shift working from Monday to Sunday of every week. One hour is accounted for lunch and breaks. If you lose 20 products because you stop the line to understand the problem and fix it, you lose 80 products in the week. However, all the products that you sent to the end of the assembly line are of good quality per your control plan. If you decide not to stop the line even for 50% of the problems, you will be sending 40 jobs to the end of the assembly line with problems expecting a repair person will fix them. Assuming that you use 40 man-hours for repair down the assembly line at $25 per hour, you will spend $1000 to repair the 40 units for a week or $50000 per year or $75000 if the repairmen are working overtime (in case of a 50% premium for overtime).

If you keep such plan of work, your workforce will become complacent and the problems will not be fixed to the root cause. By relying on repairs you open doors to potentially serious quality issues because in general repair operations are not controlled as well as the processes of the assembly line. Your workforce may not significantly reduce production losses nor improve quality but instead will be firefighting. Worst, you will not protect the customer because rework workers may still release products with defects that will reach the end customers.

You will be better off accepting that there is a state of crisis and you need to stop the line in order to learn how to improve and drive the solutions to the root cause. You may use problem solving with planned reviews at the workstation (plan do check act and Genchi Genbutsu). To have world-class quality in manufacturing, you may still have a repair or a rework area but your goal should be to drive the numbers of products that go to the repair area to zero.

2.6) Standardized tasks are the foundation for continuous improvement

Once workers are confident about the best way of doing a job then they should record the steps of the process as simply and clearly as possible in their work instruction and add visual aids or videos for illustration. They may change the standard only if they find a better way (with evidences) of doing the job, which then becomes the new standard. This is valid for an assembly plant, a bank or mortgage process, a pizza business, a hamburger fast food, a hospital emergency service, a university's degree program process, or a political party process.

2.7) Visual management and control to avoid hiding concerns

Hidden issues increase the amount of hidden wastes that may not be controlled by front line workers or dealt with by management. Rework lines or rework cells are typical drivers of hidden or overlooked issues. There may also be hidden factories all over the plant or the service location. For instance when a service provider tells you "I am doing this for you but I do not want my boss to know about it", you just witnessed a hidden factory. There is a problem that the agent does not want his boss to know about and fixing the problem without a manager or a supervisor knowing is a hidden factory.

Overtime the overlooking and hiding of issues cause chronic business losses and underperformances. Visual aids also help employees remember the most critical steps of a job.

2.8) Make sure that you use technologies that are reliable and have been proven robust

Here is an example of this principle for a service business. You have a tax business and you need to order five computers and one security software for your business. Per this principle you need to be as thorough as possible to select the most robust computer and the most robust antivirus and antimalware software for your business. You must review different rating websites, try out of different software, and benchmark computers and security software of some of your friends who own businesses. If you are introducing technology in a new product, it has to be reliable and robust or you may dissatisfy your customers or even be hit with a quality recall.

2.9) Develop leaders who thoroughly understand your business

It takes time to develop leaders who thoroughly understand your business and you need to plan for it and then execute. To really understand a business, leaders need to be passionate about it beyond the obligation of just coming to work. The critical areas of every business are: people and culture, product or service design, operations including suppliers, market and customers. You need to develop leaders who master at least one of the four areas and who still remarkably understand the three other areas. It takes hard and intelligent work, and it takes time. Understanding the business also means knowing your business capabilities and core competencies. You have to know when you need help from an outside source that may have the skills that your team does not have and does not intend to have in the future.

2.10) Develop outstanding people and teams

An organization needs a system for developing outstanding people and teams. Managers need to commit resources for developing people and teams. They also need to lead by example. Beer, a British management expert who studied strategic management and businesses as systems affirmed that managers tend to develop people who have the same profiles as their own profiles (Beer, 1974). An organization will not be very effective at developing outstanding people and team if its managers and leaders are not themselves outstanding in and great proponents and practitioners of teamwork and people development.

2.11) Respect your partners

Partners include your employees, suppliers, customers, governmental organizations, community organizations, and other business partners. An organization may not succeed unless all of the first three partners succeed. An organization will not have outstanding products or services without outstanding suppliers. If an organization avoids collaboration with its suppliers and just pushes for its needs to be fulfilled, its relationship with its suppliers will be strained overtime and the organization may miss opportunities for collaborating with its suppliers for lower costs of products or better quality. Seemingly, respecting customers means good customer service and giving customers the wants that you promised to give them. Finally, your business may not succeed if its agents and employees do not feel respected by managers and if managers do not provide the resource and conditions that allow the employees to do a good job. Besides the three first partners, an organization needs to establish good relationships with the community, government, professional organizations, universities, and other business partners in order to share knowledge and leverage various capabilities.

2.12) Go see where the problem occurs so you can better understand (Go See)

In manufacturing, business meetings should not happen only in the office. When receiving a report on an issue, there is a little bit of loss of information and the only way to learn about the issue factually is to go to the place where the issue in question occurs or had occurred. Gemba means "the real place" in Japanese. Genchi Genbutsu means "go see at the source". Gemba and Genchi Genbutsu are often used in place of Go See. In a service business such as a retail business or a fast food, a corporate director of operations is better off going to the retail store and living the experience of customers and store's workers. In automobile product development, a chief engineer should rather spend significant time reviewing prototype vehicles, tests of vehicles, or vehicle subsystems at the test sites or where the prototypes are being reviewed. Where Go See is not physically possible, engineers may use information technologies such as videos of assembly processes and videos of product tests. As reviewers observe the process, they get a better understanding and make adjustments as needed.

Managers need to follow the Deming – Shewhart cycle of continuous improvement: plan do check and act (PDCA). In a lean organization, it is better to check at Gemba which is where the problem occurs or where the process happens and mutually agree upon for a new plan with the problem solving team members. Doing so promotes coaching, learning, teamwork, and commitment to getting things done. For instance in product development, it is better for engineers and their managers to review fits or misfits of design parts on prototypes and on a simulation screen rather than to just discuss the misfits following a Microsoft PowerPoint presentation or a summary report on paper. Following the review (check step of PDCA) the team members act through problem solving and the team defines a new plan agreed upon by all (plan step of PDCA). Afterwards the team executes the plan (do step of PDCA), checks the progress made, and acts again. Seemingly, airline managers should rather review missing luggage from the cashier area at the airport, through the luggage loading area in the airplanes, through the unloading areas of airplanes, and all the way down to the release of luggage at the arrival area of the airport. The airline managers should follow a PDCA cycle relying on all the employees involved and developing their skills in order to solve problems faster.

2.13) Take time and use consensus to make decisions

For decision making, thoroughness is better than speed. Here is an example that illustrates the negative consequences of decisions made without consensus. Let us consider the head of a business called ABC Inc who is in a meeting which purpose is to select a marketing company for a needed critical market campaign. In the meeting, one of the managers believes that many potential consulting companies need to bid and the team should only make a choice after a thorough review of all the bidders. The head of the company already has his idea in mind and says "I trust Excel Marketing and their CEO is a friend, he will give us a good financial deal". The manager shuts up as he is afraid to challenge the head of the company. Excel Marketing receives an offer for the marketing campaign contract and accepts it. Unfortunately, the campaign has average results. In this case, it is clear that ABC Business did not take the time to review all the options and the selection was not optimized because the pools of potentially better deals was limited to only one vendor.

Another example is common in product development. If hasty decisions are made, the engineering team has to make many engineering changes, sometimes when the product is already in service. Consensus by many experts from different disciplines such as design, core engineering, manufacturing, quality, and marketing may take longer but helps minimize the occurrences of costly engineering changes downstream after managers freeze the design.

2.14) Grow to become a learning organization

A learning organization is self-sustained by its processes, people, and culture. It can be considered a cybernetic system where people continuously learn from challenges in order to improve the business from its current state and find new horizons and ideas to succeed in a competitive market. As an example, here are two of the Toyota's principle elaborated n 1937

1) Our customers are at the core of what we do

2) We must not be satisfied with our current state. We need to keep looking for better of ways of doing things

For Toyota, continuous improvement means relentless search for improvement added to Kaizen and Genchi Genbutsu. Kaizen's main characteristics are the acceptance of problems as opportunities for improvement relying on the people who do the jobs and whom management gives the power and means to solve problems in teams. Genchi Genbutsu is the continuous learning and solving of problems where they happen. Problems generally occur within manufacturing workstations, or where engineers do their works. Respect for people and teamwork means the company values individual contribution but emphasizes the reliance on teamwork because "we are stronger when working as a team". These three pillars of continuous improvement have enabled Toyota to continuously grow its business for the last forty years.

The fourteen Toyota Way's principles are equivalent to the eight principles mentioned earlier when I defined lean enterprise (page 3 and 4) as long as I assume realistically that problems, concerns, and outcomes of the negation of the principles are equal to waste

2.15. Exercises 2

Exercise 2.1

Think about the organization that you work for today or that you worked for in the past

Q2.1.1) Do senior managers and executives make decision for the long term?

Q2.1.2) What are the evidences that managers make decision for the long terms?

Q2.1.3) What has the company's financial performance been for the last five years

Exercise 2.2

Q2.2.1) Write an essay on your understanding of Toyota Way's principle 5

Q2.2.2) Give some examples to supports your rationale

Exercise 2.3

Q2.3.1) Explain in your own words the benefits of being a learning organization

Q2.3.2) Give an example of one learning organization. Justify your choices

Exercise 2.4

Q2.4.1) What are the signs that an enterprise is not good at continuous improvement?

Q2.4.2) Write your answer in the form of a one page essay

Chapter 3
Clarifying Lean Enterprise

3.1) What lean enterprise is versus what lean enterprise is not

Practitioners often misunderstand lean enterprise or lean manufacturing. Many managers often assume that lean enterprise means cost reduction and therefore they stretch their employees beyond the acceptable limit defined by the demand of products and services. The result is often poor decision making, incomplete work, and poor quality in general. When an enterprise has not formally adopted lean enterprise as a strategy there are often fears and misconceptions.

The Misconceptions will persist as long as senior management does not clarify what lean enterprise is and what it is not to its immediate subordinates and its subordinates do not communicate a similar message to the rest of the employees. Table 2 includes a comparative list of what lean enterprise is and what it is not, and should help managers clarify lean enterprise to their team members.

Table 2
Clarification of What Lean Enterprise Is versus What it Is not

What lean enterprise is not	What lean enterprise is
Management ruling by dictation	Coaching and leading by examples.
A recipe of Lean Tools such as Kanban, 6 Sigma, Just in Time (JIT), 5S, TPM, Visual Factory, Poke Yoke	Management by a broad consensus
Just a training taught as a lecture	Lean tools used selectively by empowered people that continuously minimize waste.
Just a display of metric data	Learning by doing and "Go-See" for deeper understanding
A continuous change of processes as Management changes	Systems accepted and supported by the whole enterprise through standardized work
Continuous fire fighting	A continuous drive to do it right the first time and to learn from past mistakes
Just Cost cutting	Effectively solving problems, thus decreasing the rate of reoccurrence
A system supported by one person or just a group of persons	A system that includes the enterprise's partners (its suppliers, employees, customers, the communities, the governments)
Just in one department: Production, Engineering, Maintenance,...etc	A system where decision are made with a long term views of potential consequences
Just a system for one facility or for an insulated company	

3.2) Lean enterprise versus organization strategy and core competencies

The enterprise core competencies define what the enterprise does best. The enterprise culture includes the enterprise core competencies and the way people interact among themselves, with their customers, their partners, the community, and the world. The organization strategy is the set of planned actions that enable the company to be competitive in a mid or long term. The enterprise's mission statement greatly influences the company's culture

Lean enterprise principles derive from the Toyota Production System (TPS). It is not wise for an enterprise to throw away its core system or principles, replacing them with lean principles. If a company is in business for some years, it means the company does something right. What is wise is to adapt lean principles to the company's core competencies and strategies with a set of tools and procedures that are company specific.

Exercise 3.1
Q3.2.1) Find one company on the internet that has its annual report and sustainability report on the internet.
Q3.2.2) What is the company mission statement? Does the mission statement include any of the Toyota way's 14 principles? If yes list the principles?
Q3.2.3) Summarize the company core strategy and leadership principles.
Q3.2.4) Do the strategy and leadership principles include any of the 14 Toyota Way's principles?

Exercise 3.2
Q3.2.1) In your own words explain how the 14 Toyota principles can help a bank. Your answer must be a one page essay
Q3.2.2) Do banks have products? If yes list five of them

Exercise 3.3
Q3.2.1) In your own words explain how the 14 Toyota principles can help a government. Your answer must be a one page essay

Exercise 3.4
Your answer must be a two to three pages essay
Google and search information about ISO principles. List the principles
Compare the ISO Principles with the 14 Toyota Way's principles. ISO stands for International Standard Organization.

Exercise 3.5
Your answer must be a two to three pages essay
Google and search information about Total Quality Management (TQM). List the principles
Compare the total quality management principles with the 14 Toyota Way's principles

3.3) Benefits of Lean Enterprise when Lean Is Effective

3.3.1) Better deals between the Union and the organization

In a lean enterprise there are better deals and better relationships between managers and the union because the company's agents respect the union which is an important partner, develop their employees, take time to develop leaders who understand their business, and decide for the long term. In an effective lean enterprise, non union employees collaborate with the union members and the union leaders and usually the union and the company try to find a common ground so they can mutually benefit. However, it is up to the enterprise's managers to lead by clarifying what is at stake which is often the success and survival of the business. An effective lean enterprise involves its people in waste reduction efforts and ensures that union members grow in different positions within the organization. When union members get involved in the business they feel valued, become more skillful employees, and achieve better business results.

3.3.2) Compliance to the organization code of conduct by all employees

In a lean enterprise, there is compliance to the enterprise's code of conduct because there is respect for all employees and among all employees, employees work to minimize the wastes from non compliance to the company's code of conduct, and because management makes decisions for the long terms. However, for all employees to comply with the code of conduct managers will have to ensure accountability for misbehaviors for all employees regardless of whether they belong or they do not belong to the union and regardless of their position. Managers also have to lead by example otherwise employees may no longer trust them or believe in the code of conduct.

3.3.3) Minimization of the risk to make products that customers do not want

In a lean enterprise managers minimize the risk to make products that the customers do not want because of a robust pull system and because employees relentlessly work on minimizing wastes from quality defects and rework, take the time to fix problems, make sure that the technologies they add in products or services are robust, and drive continuous improvement using Gemba, kaizen and employee involvement. By not becoming comfortable with the status quo, employees consider quality defects as challenges they can overcome and solve in teams, which leads to better quality compared to the competitors

3.3.4) Increased innovation as long as the organization develops innovative agents

Innovative agents are the people who make innovation happen. They may be engineers, researchers, scientists, market analysts, brainstorming and creativity facilitators, senior managers, and leaders. They may also be members of a union. Innovation is necessary in order to make the fourteenth principle of the Toyota way possible, meaning for the company to become a learning organization. As the company learns from the market and as the market changes a company without creativity will not be able to continuously adapt to new customers or new market, becoming vulnerable to competitors. The selection of innovative agents has to be fair and equitable otherwise wrong people will be selected and there will be waste from poor utilization of human capital triggered by waste from non compliance to the company's code of conduct. The code of conduct in question here is integrity and fairness in the promotion and the development of employees. Great lean companies such as Toyota, Honda, or Intel have a record of developing good innovative agents because they do so with integrity and equity.

3.3.5) Minimization of critical risks such as recalls and safety casualties

Because lean enterprise requires taking the time to fix problems then managers provides the workforce with the tools and other resources that enable them to control quality with robust design and in-process control tools such as autonomation, Poka Yoke, and standardization. Employees are working in problem solving teams around their jobs and management provides support by going to see at the workstation where problems occur. I have stressed the night waste which is the waste from non compliance to code of conducts because throughout the first half of the 2010s, recalls that could have been solved easily were worsened because managers or engineers decided to cover up quality issues that they knew about. By understanding that such behaviors lead to wastes that sometimes cost companies billions of dollars lean focused organization will give their employees training, audits, and governance so they employees can adopt lean behaviors.

3.3.6) Higher return to shareholders over time

Returns to shareholders depend on how the enterprise pays its shareholders. For instance, some public companies do not pay dividends even though the companies remain profitable and realize positive cash flows. The only positive return for a common stock investor in such cases will be from an eventual growth of the stock value. Companies such as Honda, Intel, and Toyota have realized positive returns in terms of returned earnings or dividends steadily for from the 1980s to the years 2000s. The reasons why lean enterprise drives positive financial results when a company's workforce follows the principles is that lean enterprise stresses consensual and long term decision making, and scalability driven by a pull system of production or service delivery, minimum inventory, and reduction of waste. With lean enterprise, a business makes sure that the unit cost of each product is low enough compared to the price of the products to generate positive acceptable returns.

3.3.7) Better work life and job balance

Because lean enterprise requires the respect and development of employees, employees will find the opportunities to have their voices heard on issues that affect employee morale and on suggestions for continuous improvement, and will be able to contribute to problem solving. Lean enterprises open doors to employees of all background considering their individual capabilities, offering them the opportunities to work in result driven teams, and to receive coaching from management in kaizen events.

3.3.8) Better relationship with the network of suppliers and better performance of suppliers

Because lean enterprise calls for respect of partners, a lean company selects its suppliers by assessing their capabilities. Afterwards, a lean enterprise nurtures a win-win relationship because the success of the supplier depends on the success of the company outsourcing its products and vice versa. Business customers and their suppliers often organize themselves in network of tier two suppliers, tier one suppliers, and the customer. Within networks of suppliers, joint teams develop products together while sharing knowledge that enables the improvement of operational performance. The manufacturer often assists its suppliers in quality improvement and cost reduction, allowing the suppliers to make profits while benefiting from purchased products at a lower cost and better quality.

3.3.9) The organization becomes a learning organization

As a lean enterprise, employees focus on continuous improvement working in teams and receiving the development needed to do jobs in which they are empowered to give their inputs for standardization and problem solving. In a long run, employees become confident that they can rise to challenges and resolve problems such as quality defects, launches of new products under competitive pressure, safety concerns, or unwanted costs. In such companies, employees do not panic because they know they have individual skills and can come together to resolve ongoing concerns. The company becomes a learning organization, which means a company that is self-adaptive, relying on its people and on their ability to learn, solve problems, and considering knowledge as a core capability.

Consequently, there are other benefits resulting from the benefits that I just listed and from the fourteen lean principles such as: better quality, higher customer satisfaction, a stronger brand value, minimum waste of resources, greater inventory turnover, lower employee turnover, and better sales volumes. Better sales volumes mean resources are scaled to sales volumes which are scaled to demand. Better sales volumes do not mean higher sales volumes. If demand is 90,000 units then we plan to produce about 90,000 units for resources costing 810,000 dollars then when demand decreases to 80,000 units we must plan for producing 80,000 units for resources of costing about 720,000 dollars assuming a liner relationship between costs and outputs.

3.4) Barriers to Lean Enterprise

3.4.1) Absence of leadership buy-off

Without management buy-off it will be difficult to deploy lean enterprise or to have all the needed resources for maintaining lean enterprise. Senior executives also set the cadence for lean enterprise by defining when and where lean enterprise will be deployed first, how managers will progressively deploy lean enterprise in each division, and who the partners for lean enterprise will be. Without the chief executive's buy-off lean enterprise may not be aligned to the corporate strategy in all the divisions.

3.4.2) Potential misinterpretation of lean enterprise

Managers may consider lean enterprise as a set of lean tools only. They may consider lean enterprise as a cost reduction effort only. They may also consider lean enterprise as a set of processes or principles to be pushed top down without empowering people doing value adding jobs. Another misconception is to have managers apply lean enterprise in manufacturing without applying it to product development. When managers embrace such misconception and when they fails to consider the need for building a supporting culture and a supporting structure for lean enterprise that both involve empowered workers, teamwork, problem solving at the place where workers add value to the product or service, lean enterprise will fail to deliver the expected benefits. Many of the lean Six Sigma trainings emphasize sets of lean tools and Six Sigma tools without spending much time on the cultural and people side of lean which are arguably the most important. As experienced in many accompanies such as Toyota, Honda, and Ford Motor Company, it takes time to build a lean culture and doing so happens through a combination of ongoing training, ongoing teamwork, and the usage of lean tools incrementally and continuously over time.

3.4.3) Lack of continuity.

In some organizations, the head of the organization may lead the implementation of lean enterprise but when he or she leaves for another job, the new manager brings in new processes that replace the old ones. In such cases, the workforce becomes confused and may feel betrayed because many employees have invested a lot of the time in the old processes. If such lack of continuity prevails over time it will become difficult for the organization to mature as a learning organization.

3.4.4) Management may tolerate waste or not providing training resources

If managers tolerate waste, the rest of the workforce will follow and will believe that waste is normal in the current business. One of the wastes that managers tolerate the most is quality defect and rework waste. In manufacturing, it is common to have repair or rework workstations that are almost full of worker every day. Another common waste is inventory since many businesses may still use a push system even though they claim to be lean. Having managers not following a cycle of continuous improvement combined with problem solving and teamwork also hinders the transformation of an organization into a lean enterprise.

3.4.5) Presence of resistance to change combined with management giving up

Change is difficult and it is more difficult when there is open resistance to change. There are employees who may resist to lean transformation because they wrongly believe that they may lose their job or will not be able to adapt. Usually when they have not received good communication of the benefits of lean for themselves such as better work life balance and a more financially stable business, high seniority workers may resist to change. There are also people who resist to changes because of their mindset of not being open to get out of their comfort zone. It is the role of managers to build confidence in the people who resist to lean transformation through dialogue and open communication, and when possible by giving a list of examples of lean successes in organizations that are similar in size and business line to their own organization. If managers give up on lean transformation then the transformation into a lean organization will not be successful.

3.4.6) A top down culture or a command and control culture

A top down culture with many management levels is an opposite to the inclusion of workers to solve problems altogether with managers in problem solving teams. Because lean requires respect for and development of people it implies an open dialogue and people empowerment without continuously waiting for instructions from their bosses. In a top down culture, unless senior managers initially train managers on they need to progressively transition towards a flatter structure and they need to empower people, lean transformation will fail.

3.4.7) Presence of silos where the enterprise does not behave as one team

A lean enterprise needs unity toward business goals, thus silos hinders transformation to lean because of their risk to drive the workforce in two or more business directions. Silos entertain unnecessary reliance on self interests away from the common interest of the organization. Lean transformation is a serious goal because it is at the core of the organization strategy, thus senior executives, senior managers, and managers should break silos if they want to maximize the probability for having lean transformation successful.

Chapter 4
The Concept of Waste

4.1) Definition of waste

A waste is any action that does not add nor contribute to value for the customer. Value here means the customer expected experience in term of satisfaction for quality and cost. Experience here means the fulfillment of a function or a service for the customer. One should notice the word "expected" which means that a customer has to expect some features in the products or services. Customer expectations justified the segmentation of customer wants. A customer buying a mass market vehicle does not expect luxurious features in it. Passengers who purchased airline tickets of an economic class do not expect the flight attendants to give them first class accommodations. If the flight attendants give economic passengers a first class service, it will be waste for the airline.

To identify waste, it is necessary to break down the process in individual elements in order to identify activities that add value versus activities that do not add value. A task is necessary when based on the physical and process constraints employees cannot complete the job without completing the task in question.

Example 4.1.
Burger (hamburger assembly) process at Jerry Burger LLC

You go to Jerry Burger to order a Great Jerry Burger. You order the sandwich requesting tomatoes, onions, mayonnaise, no pickle, and no lettuce.

Here is the process at Jerry Burger

Process Steps
1) Grab ten pieces of sliced buns and place it open in the oven.
2) Grab a piece of Great Jerry hamburger and place it in a baking tray
3) Place the baking tray in the oven
4) Leave tray in the oven at 350 degrees F for two minutes.
5) Remove the ten pieces of bun from the oven after two minutes
6) Remove the hamburger from the oven after four minutes
7) Grab about five slices of onions and place them on top of the hamburger
8) Spread the mayonnaise on top of the hamburger and onion assembly
9) Place two slices of tomatoes on top of the hamburger and onion assembly
10) Place the hamburger assembly between the two half pieces of buns
11) Grab a Great Jerry box and open the box
12) Place the hamburger in the box and close the box
13) Grab a medium size cardboard bag and place the box into the bag top up
14) Grab two napkins, one plastic knife, and one plastic fork in the bag.
15) Pass the bag to the delivery person by the second window
16) Pass the bag to the customer

4.2) Value adding and non value adding activities

Waste is any activity within a business process that does not add value to the product or to the service meanwhile value is anything that fulfills the customer expected experience in term of quality and cost. There are activities that add values and activities that do not add value. I am giving below four examples (example four to five) to help readers easily classify the activities in their business setting or in their organization. I am also listing two exercises and three problems that readers may resolve for training themselves. I am listing the problems just after the second exercise.

Value adding tasks that are necessary do not contribute to waste while non value adding tasks may contribute to waste. Some value adding tasks may be unnecessary when they are redundant; in that case they are waste (called over-processing waste)

Waste derives from non value adding activities but some wastes are necessary and managers need to remove them as much as possible but managers need to completely eliminate unnecessary waste.

Example 4.2
Hamburger assembly at Jerry Burger: Value adding activities identified

The bun, the hamburger, the onions, and the tomatoes contribute to value. Seemingly having the oven at 350 degree F contributes to value because it helps hit the buns and bake the hamburger for a good taste. Now if the burger maker adds pickles or lettuce to the burger, he or she will be adding waste because the customer does not expect lettuce or pickles. Seemingly, if onions or tomatoes are too ripe with a bad taste and get added to the sandwich, there will be waste. When the burger maker walks to deliver the burger to the order and delivery person, many of the steps are waste but many are also necessary. The manager can had a sliding rail to feed the burgers immediately to the order delivery person set next to the pick up windows. Such act if completed will eliminate motion waste realized by the burger maker. Here are all the steps.

Process Steps
1) Grab ten pieces of sliced buns and place it open in the oven. The task is non value adding but necessary. There may be waste if there are left over of buns at the end of the shift.

2) Grab a piece of Great Jerry hamburger and place it in a baking tray. The task is non value adding but necessary. There is no waste as long as there is no unnecessary delay before placing the tray in the oven. There will be waste if the hamburger maker has to walk unnecessarily.

3) Place the baking tray in the oven. The task is non value adding but necessary

4) Leave tray in the oven at 350 degrees F for two minutes. The task is value adding and necessary

5) Remove the ten pieces of bun from the oven after two minutes. The task is value adding and necessary but there will be waste if the bun stays in the oven longer than two minutes.

6) Remove the hamburger from the oven after four minutes. The task is value adding and necessary but if you removed it after exactly three minutes or exactly five minutes, you have a defect even if the customer accepts the hamburger.

7) Grab five slices of onions and place them on top of the hamburger. The task is value adding and necessary

8) Spread the mayonnaise circularly on top of the hamburger and onion assembly. The task is value adding and necessary

9) Place two slices of tomatoes on top of the hamburger and onion assembly. The task is value adding and necessary. If the burger maker places three slices of tomatoes in the sandwich, there will be a waste of one slice that waste of over processing that is a subject of discussion in subsequent pages of this book.

10) Place the hamburger assembly between the two half-pieces of buns. You have a sandwich made. The task is value adding and necessary

11) Grab a Great Jerry box and open the box. The task is value adding and necessary because the customer expects the sandwich inside a box but the actual boxes used may be too costly thus unnecessary as long there are cheaper substitute available.

12) Place the hamburger in the box and close the box. The task is value adding and necessary. Yes it is value adding because the customer expects the hamburger in a box. It is part of the customer's experience

13) Grab a medium size cardboard bag and place the box into the bag top up. The task is value adding and necessary

14) Grab two napkins, one plastic knife, and one plastic fork in the bag. The task is value adding and necessary

15) Pass the bag to the delivery person by the second window. The task is non value adding but necessary. Need to be refined. There may be non value adding walking steps but some of the steps are necessary. The operating team at Jerry Burger should be working on minimizing the non value adding and unnecessary steps.

16) Pass the bag to the customer. The task is value adding and necessary because the customer has to get the sandwich. There may be waste if the customer has to wait too long, thus becomes dissatisfied with the service

Example 4.3
Arrival and treatment of patients in an emergency care

Process steps
1) Patients arrive at the Emergency Care and direct themselves to the registering agent. The task is non value adding but necessary. This step is not value adding to the patient's state of illness

2) The registering agent decides on the severity of the case among critical, serious, and normal cases. The task is non value adding but necessary

3) The agent sends serious and critical patients immediately to either surgery or intensive care. The task is non value adding but necessary

4) For serious and critical cases, if there is no doctor or nurse the patient waits. This task is non value adding and not necessary, this is waste and the patient health is more at risk. This is a urgent problem to be solved

5) For serious and critical cases, as soon as a doctor or a nurse is available, either or both give treatments to the patient. This task is value adding and necessary. There is a need for problem solving and someone has to be there all the time

6) For normal cases, the agent asks the patient to wait and the patient waits. The task is non value adding and not necessary. This is another unwanted state. There is a need for problem solving

7) For normal cases as soon as a space is available, the agent registers the patient and directs the patient to a patient room. The task is non value adding but necessary

8) For normal cases, a nurse first visits the patient to take more information. The task is non value adding but necessary

9) The patient waits for a doctor. The task is non value adding and not necessary. This again is waste.

10) For normal cases, the doctors examine and treat the patient. The task is value adding and necessary

11) For all cases after the doctors and nurses give treatment to the patient, the patient stays in a room for observation and further treatment. The task is value adding and necessary but there may be waste if the patient stays at the hospital longer than necessary.

12) When doctors judge the patient's health good enough, they release the patient who goes home or to a specialized hospital. The task is bon value adding but necessary. If the doctors are right ` about their assessment of the patient health, there will be value to the patient downstream but if they are wrong, there will be waste.

Example 4.4
Molding of a plastic plate

Process Steps
1) A maintenance technician reviews the production plan, cleans up the molding machine, and performs preventive maintenance. The task is non value adding but necessary

2) A production technician sets up the molding machine for pressure, cycle time, and temperature, and other parameters. The task is non value adding but necessary

3) While setting up the molding equipment, the production technician dumps plastic material as waste. The task is non value adding but necessary. Such waste needs to be minimized or controlled

4) A production worker reviews the product plan and verifies that the production leader has correctly set up the molding equipment; such verification includes verification of raw material consistency. The task is non value adding but necessary

5) The production worker runs the mold cycle after cycle. The task is value adding and necessary

6) For each cycle, the production worker verifies cycle completion, and removes flashes. The task is non value adding but necessary

7) For each cycle, the production worker verifies the quality of the product for each cavity, discards defective parts in the red storage bin reserved for defective parts. The task is non value adding but necessary

8) The production worker calls a production leader or maintenance when he or she notices an abnormality. The task is non value adding but necessary. However the number of such calls need to be minimized

9) The production worker records abnormalities, counts of defective parts, the types of defective parts, and the counts of good parts every hour on the assigned record workbook for traceability and further problem solving. This task is non value adding but necessary

10) A production leader reviews compliance to processes at the workstation for every shift. The task is non value adding but necessary

11) A production supervisor and a quality engineer review compliance to processes for each shift respectively once per week and once per month. The task is non value adding but necessary

Example 4.5
Design of a more stable manual car jack

Process Steps
1) Engineers and sales professionals gather data from customers, current vehicle weights, and currently sold car jacks. This is value adding and necessary. Missing the correct customer' requirements will result to waste. This is a task on which professionals identify what value is for the customer. They will have to confirm and communicate the value to the customer after the make the products, thus for the customer it will become expected value.

2) Engineers use the data to create design requirements. This task is value adding and necessary.

3) Design engineers, material experts, and manufacturing engineers meet to define the initial concept of the jack. This task is value adding and necessary. There may be waste if wrong decision are made but are not identified

4) Engineers, material experts, manufacturing engineers meet again to finalize the initial design. This task is value adding and necessary

5) The team finalizes analytical design verification for fatigue under distributed cycles. This task is non value adding but necessary

6) The design team verifies resistance to static loads using linear and non-linear finite element analyses. This task is non value adding but necessary. The design team creates value here but it should minimize the risk of not satisfying the end customer.

7) The design team builds the prototype in house or outsources the build of prototypes. This task is value adding. The customers here are the manufacturing team and the end customer

8) The design team performs functional, static, and dynamic testing using prototypes. This task is non value adding but necessary

9) The manufacturing team builds production prototypes and the design team uses them to adjust the design. This task is value adding and necessary

10) The design team finalizes drawings and bills of material and the design is ready for production. The task is non value adding activity and necessary

Problem 1: Assembly of calipers to disk brakes
Determine which activity is value adding and necessary, value adding but not necessary, non value adding but necessary, or non value adding and not necessary

Process Steps.

1) The production operator verifies the sequencing or A, B, C for caliper A, B, or C; and R for drum brakes.

2) If the order is R for drum brakes, the worker does nothing.

3) When the number of calipers at the workstation falls below 5 for any type or caliper, the production operator calls a production leader to fill in more calipers for covering two hour of production.

4) Grab a caliper and hose assembly and verify that the type of hose assembled matches the caliper.

5) Insert the caliper pad opening around the disk brake at the top of the disk.

6) Insert a bolt between the caliper bracket and the axle bracket hole.

7) Tighten the bolt with a CAN 3 T torque gun.

8) If the line stops, it means that the bolt is either cross-threaded or the specified torque has not been reached. In that case you must unbolt the assembly using one of three manual torque wrenches A, B, and C that matches each of the assembly, discard the first bold in a red bin, and reassemble with a new bolt using the CAN 3 T torque gun.

9) If the line stops again for the same axle, release the axle, flag it with a red metallic flag, and call your group leader.

10) Record all reworks in the abnormality event log book

11) Group leader, production supervisor, production manager, and quality auditor/manager review compliance to standard respectively daily, weekly, monthly, and quarterly.

Problem 2: Development of a new cellular phone

A cellular telephone company named Star Electronics has brought to the market a cellular telephone named Starphone, but customers are not buying as many Starphone units as planned. Start Electronics has even thought about discontinuing the telephone but the suppliers and retailers have raised their disagreements. Star Electronics decides to quickly redesign a new telephone called Starphone 2 using feedback from customers and competitor benchmark. Star Electronics gives itself nine months to bring Starphone 2 to the market.

Determine which activity is value adding and necessary, value adding but not necessary, non value adding but necessary, or non value adding and not necessary

Process Steps

1) Engineers and sales professionals gather data from customers and competitors' cellular phones.

2) Engineers use the data to update design requirements.

3) The design team meets to finalize the initial design.

4) The design team verifies durability and function using simulation, analytics, and engineering judgment, as well as the initial prototypes.

5) The design team builds second stage prototypes relying on its pilot team and its suppliers and using production tools.

6) The design team performs functional, static, and dynamic testing on production prototypes

7) The design team makes adjustments as needed.

8) The manufacturing team builds more production prototypes

9) The design team uses them to adjust the design and Star electronic proposes them to selected customers for trials.

10) The design team finalizes drawings and bills of material and the design is ready for production using feedback from the trial. The design is ready for launch

Problem 3: Collection of parking ticket throughout a city

A city office manager assigns two collectors per shift for each of the five different areas of the city. The collectors work from 7:00 AM to 4:30 PM and cannot go on break simultaneously. The collector's job is to assign a ticket to each vehicle that is wrongly parked or parked too long per assigned city's ordinances. Out of the five collectors, a few starts having behaviors that did comply with the process. Some of them would go on break for too long, which cause them not to cover all the parking spots. Others would give breaks to vehicles owners who should normally receive a ticket at the exchange of a bribe valued at about 25% of the fine. Here, the collectors follow a process that deviates from the prescribed process.

Determine which activity is value adding and necessary, value adding but not necessary, non value adding but necessary, or non value adding and not necessary

Process steps

1) Report to work at 7:00 AM in the morning.
2) Drive a vehicle to parking spots.
3) Identify a vehicle that should receive a ticket.
4) Assign a ticket to the vehicle.
5) Go on break.
6) Return from break,
7) Repeat steps 3) and 4).
8) Report the list of tickets to the city clerk.
9) Go home.
10) The owners' of vehicles that receive the ticket pay the fine.
11) The city clerk collects the fine.

4.3) Summary of value adding versus non value adding activities

We can prioritize activities this way when we are looking for waste reduction opportunities

4.3.1) Non value adding and unnecessary activities

These activities are waste that must be eliminated. They are often a result of unwanted conditions driven by operational constraints. In the emergency room example, having nurses and doctors not available when needed is an example of such activities. The purpose of an emergency room is to treat people who need immediate care. Had emergency care patients been able to wait, they would have waited for visiting a doctor in a non emergency care or clinic in the next day. Hence seeing a doctor in an emergency care is a necessity. In a regular clinic or a regular hospital, there may be a constraint of limited budget and many doctors may not be available otherwise the clinic or the hospital may never break even financially. In such a case the activity of having a patient wait for a doctor is non value adding but necessary. I have just illustrated the importance of taking into account the business context, the business constraints, and business boundaries when analyzing activities in terms of value adding and non value adding activities.

4.3.2) Value adding but unnecessary activities

These are redundant activities that cause over-processing waste. They may not be easy to identify but the process or design team needs to review every value adding activity for redundancy. Avoid adding unnecessary and costly value to the customers which is over-quality that the customer does not pay for. Value is about customer expectations. Examples are offering luxurious seats or features in a mass vehicle and offering first class accommodations and products to airline passengers of the economic class. Customers of the economic class do not expect first class accommodations. If the airline keeps offering economic class customers first class accommodations, it may initially attract more customers to its economic class but quite surely it number of first class customers will decrease. Such proceeding will lead to confusion between the two classes and the airline will more likely realize negative cash flows.

4.3.3) Non value adding but necessary activities

These activities may still need to be reviewed as there may still be waste in it. Some of them may also be redundant. Is there a way to eliminate such activities? I already gave one example in the discussion of 7.3.1) about non value adding and unnecessary activities. The example is that of patients waiting in a regular clinic or a regular hospital. In the view of the customer, the expectation is to see a doctor while expecting some level of waiting time. However the primary expectation is to see a doctor. The question is: does the customer has to wait? The answer is yes because the hospital has a limited number of doctors and in this case, the wait may not endanger the health of the patient beyond the symptoms that led the customer to decide to visit a doctor. Non value adding but necessary activities are the reality of many business operations and usually require allocation of resources in order to be eliminated. In the case just discussed, the hospital may hire doctorate of medicine students on call at a lower cost than that of regular doctors to cover for spikes in demand which are instances of many more patients visiting doctors. Doing so will minimize waiting time.

4.3.4) Value adding and necessary activities

These are the activities that add value and the team should keep them in control. A value adding and necessary activity may still generate waste of poor quality (rework and defects) or delay when an equipment breakdown or if there is a missing worker at the job. Most people have been in a store to find out that there in an uncommon queue waiting to cash out in front of one cashier. It is waste for the customer because the customer does not expect to wait for an excessively long time. Cashing out is a value adding activity for the process of purchasing since without purchasing the customer will not own the product or complete the service being purchased. Cashing out is also a necessary activity as the closure of the purchase. However similar to the example of a manufacturing operation, there is waste within the cashing out activity. When waiting lines are too long, some customers will exit the store and go to the next store and the store will lose profit margins.

Chapter 5
Classifying Waste

There were seven main wastes identified in lean manufacturing from the 1980 throughout the early 2000s as enunciated by Taiichi Ohno of Toyota Motor Company (Ohno, 1988). Since the second half of the 2000s years, practitioners of lean enterprise have acknowledge the eighth waste which is the waste of poor utilization of human and intellectual resources . I will be going through the different eight wastes, I will break down two of the wastes, each in two different types, I will add a new type of waste, and I will present different examples, exercises, or cases on each of them.

5.1) Motion waste

5.1.1) Definition of motion waste
Motion waste is waste which is a result of workers' unnecessary bending, reaching, walking, twisting, turning, or searching for tools. In production or services, processing time is increased by unnecessary walking out of the walking space, thus decreasing throughput, and often getting the worker tired (defects, mistakes, injuries).

5.1.2) Example of motion waste

Example a)
Unnecessary walking, bending or turning on an assembly line

Example b)
A printer or copier located on a non optimal place in a business office causing business officers to walk extensively in order to make copies.

Example c)
A soccer team forward has to stay up front and not waste his energy running too far back to defend.

5.1.3) Causes of motion waste
Unnecessary walking may be the result of a poor design of the working space, in offices, or in product development. In manufacturing there may be unnecessary bending, turning, or grabbing that may increase the job cycle time or cause injuries. In office or in product development workers may be walking too far to make copies or to attend a frequent meeting. If the engineers spend 30 minutes daily just walking to make copies and another 40 minutes to get into the meeting rooms, the total accounts for 70 minutes per day or 280 minutes for four days of work and 350 minutes for five days of work . Engineers are spending between four hours and 40 minutes and five hours and 50 minutes just walking to go meetings or to make copies. A better design of meeting rooms and copy rooms may save engineers at least four hours per weeks which they can use to design system components. Industrial engineers, manufacturing engineers, and process experts need to work together in order to design job with minimum motion waste.

5.1.4) Consequences of motion waste

Motion wastes unnecessarily increase the cycle times of manufacturing and services jobs and lead to lost time for doing value adding jobs in an office environment. The waste may also lead to injuries, a consequence of poor ergonomics as workers stretch their arms, twist their bodies, or excessively bend. Injuries may lead to poor morale, workers being absent from work, and higher labor costs. Motion waste also leads to poor quality as a consequence of poor ergonomics and shorter times to do value adding work

5.1.5) Solutions to motion waste

Value stream mapping which I will discuss in module 2 enables to identify non value adding activities in a process flow and to modify the initial process flow map to a new one with less non value adding activities. Using value stream mapping may help determine actives with have excessive and unnecessary people motion. Another activity that may help design a better job once a job has been identified as a job with excessive motion is team problem solving in Kaizen events.

Such meetings should include three among industrial engineers, process experts, ergonomics experts, tooling experts, and manufacturing engineers. The problem solving team should also include at least one of the people who have done the job regularly as their inputs represent the daily concern of the average worker on the job. The main goal when designing or redesigning a job is to ensure that workers remain in their natural working space which is the working space with minimum bending, stretching, walking, or twisting.

Involving the people that perform the job in completing value stream mapping and job analyses is a determinant of success because engineers alone may not have the practical feeling of handling tools when the worker is on a learning curve at the job. Unfortunately many job redesign activities for new usually lack the presence of a person who has done a job similar to the job being designed. In such unfortunate cases, quality problems and downtimes arise during the launch of the product.

Once a problem solving team eliminates motion waste from the process, the immediate result is often an improvement in throughput and quality. Such improvement leads to reduced cost of product per unit, reduced cost of service per unit, and savings in working capital which all contribute positively to differential cash flows. Overtime, the brand equity of the business either increases or gets protected from deterioration.

5.1.6) Exercises on people motion waste

Group or individual exercise on motion waste 1

Think about a fast food restaurant such as McDonald, Burger King, or Kentucky Fried Chicken. Focus on their drive-through serving process. Use the sketch below for illustration.

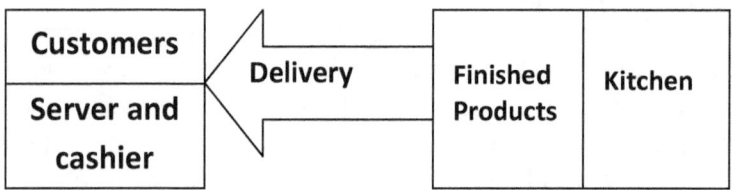

Figure 3. A View of the Delivery of Sandwiches in a Fast Food Store

Q1.1) If servers have to walk to get finished products, give an estimate of the percentage of walking time over their available working time assuming that they have three drive-through orders per minute. The average time for one order is 2 minutes. The walking distance is 10 feet (three meters). The average walking speed is six kilometers per hour.

Group or individual exercise on motion waste 2
Think about a customer bank (not a business bank). The bank has two financial agents (not the tellers) who serve customers on diverse business matters. When customers come in they sign in a log book. The agent who is free stands up then walks to read the name of the next customer to be served.

Q2.1) Write the process steps of the work done by the customer agent including the moves of the customer.

Q2.2) List any non value adding activity

Q2.3) Is there any motion waste?

Q2.4) How can the process here discussed be improved upon?

Group or individual exercise on motion waste 3
Think about your work.

Q3.1) Identify any motion waste within a business process on the floor or in office.

Q3.2) Draw a process flow chart for the process in question. Standard for the process flow chart: To represents an inspection, use a square, for work such as assembly or else, use a circle, for choice or decision, use a diamond, and for storage use an inverted triangle.

Q3.3) Give two to five ideas of improvement that could help eliminate the motion waste identified.

5.1.7 Case on people motion waste

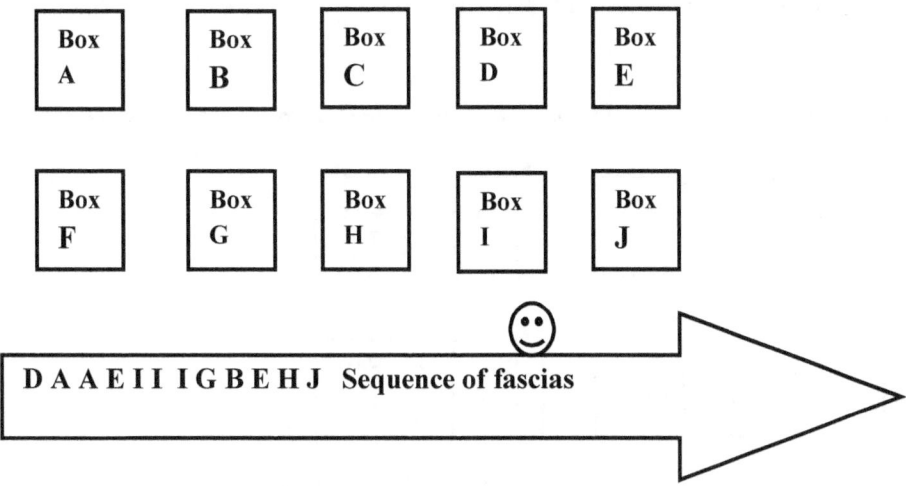

Figure 4. Current State of the Workstation

The picture above shows a workstation with one operator who assembles rear fascias on a car. There are 10 different fascias. Fascias are the plastic covers of a vehicle's bumper. A lift truck driver brings skids of fascias to the staging areas located next to the workstation. The working group has worked with industrial engineers to determine the frequencies of each kind of fascia. The most frequent fascias F, G, H, I, and J are placed up front closer to the assembly line. The least frequent ones, fascias A, B, C, D, and E are placed further. The arrows show the sequence of fascias and the direction of the work-in-process. The assembly plant had just launched the current model year version of this vehicle. However, the operator has not been able to keep up with the line speed. When industrial engineers measured the line speed, they organized labor union believed that the line was slower, unfortunately management disagreed and still disagrees. The cycle time for one operator is supposed to be 48 jobs per hour. There are 24 fascias per box.

Tony Holmes, the group leader had been working with management on process improvement for the group of twelve jobs surrounding the fascia assembly. The Manager, Les Coleman decided to call for a problem solving meeting, which is in other words, a Kaizen event. The Kaizen event had included an industrial engineer, a maintenance supervisor, a quality engineer, the zone supervisor, a union's quality representative, two operators who have worked on the fascia job in the past, Tony Holmes, and Les Coleman. The team came up with two options:

31

Option 1

Adding another worker and giving the two workers additional assembly tasks The rack closest to the operators is located 5 ft from the vehicle. The furthest one is located at 40 ft.

Option 1

Current layout of the workstation. Two operators pick up parts from the boxes.

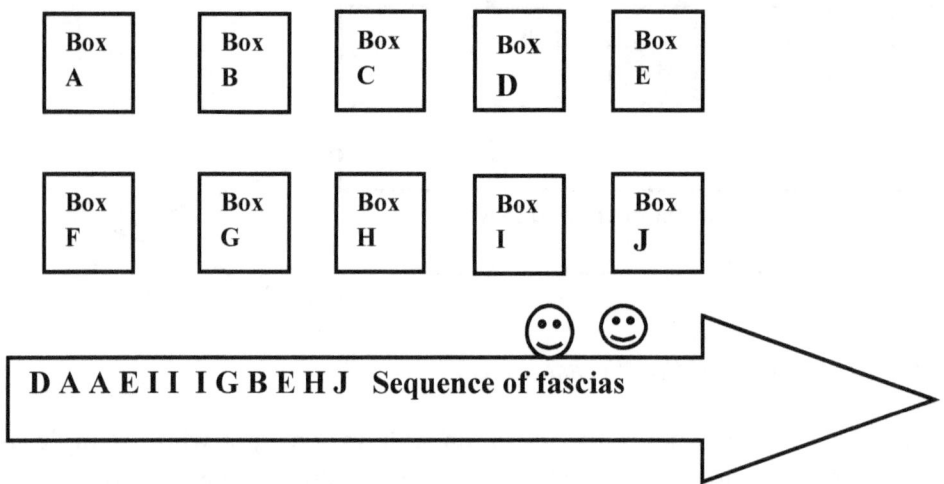

Figure 5. A View of Option 1

Option 2

A third operator picks up parts from boxes and places them in sequence on the two racks. The two assembly operators do not have to walk.

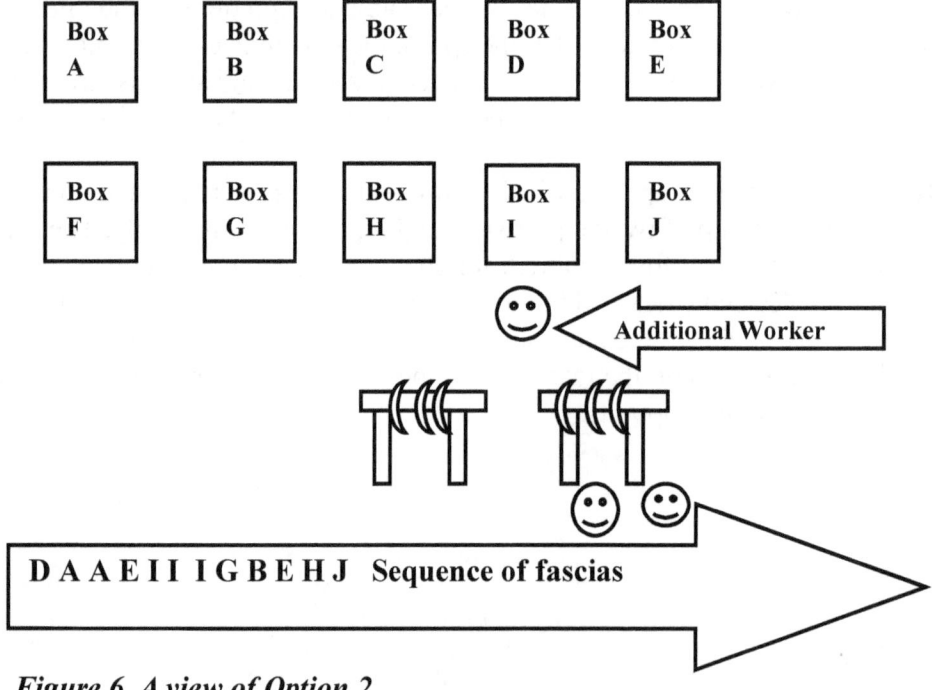

Figure 6. A view of Option 2

Adding two racks to the workstation and having a feeding operator feed the racks in sequence per the figure displayed above. The racks are located 5 feet from the vehicle. The feeding operator will be feeding two other workstations with different parts. Thus, this option adds a third of operator (1/3). Because of sequencing, discipline will be needed to avoid sequencing mistakes since the opportunities for wrong choices are now doubled. Other cons of this solution are the feeding of the racks that may lead to fascia damages.

Note: The additional operator brings the parts to the rack, the two assemblers then minimize their walking distance within every cycle and throughout the shift (production period).

Q1) Working as a team, which solution would you chose?

Q2) Explain the reason why you selected the solution

Hint: Appraise the amount of waste in term of production time and in monetary amount.

5.2) Overproduction waste

5.2.1) Definition of overproduction

Overproduction waste is waste that results from producing more products than the customer needs. In such cases, managers decide to produce without a purchase order or more than the purchase order calls for. In many cases many expect to hold inventory that eventual customers may purchase later.

5.2.2) Examples of overproduction waste

Example a)

On a push manufacturing operation, many products are made, not all of them have customers. The products that do not have customers will have to be stored waiting for orders

.

Example b)

A bakery makes the same volume of French bread from Monday to Friday of every week. On a Wednesday of a current week, only 70% of the French bread made is sold.

Example c)

An automobile manufacturer is subject to drastic attacks from its competitors for one its vehicles manufactured in plant A. Plant A keep producing 900 vehicles per day. At the end of the months 18000 vehicles are produced while for the next 3 months only 12000 vehicles are sold per month.

5.2.3) Causes of overproduction waste

Overproduction may result from a flawed voice of the customer. In such cases, the enterprise's production planners mistakenly understand customers' wants in terms of volumes or decides deliberately to overproduce expecting to have many customers for their products through rebates. The lean principle missing in this case is production planning under a pull system and if using estimate of future production volumes, overproduction will mean that the forecasting model being used is not as accurate as it should be in order to avoid significant overproduction.

Managers may be under pressure from senior executives to deliver volumes of products and in such a case as already stated managers will deliberately use a push system. The planning may be poor for other reasons than the non accuracy of the forecasting system. Assumptions for the forecasting systems may not be realistic enough. Poor communication among production planners, sales, distributors, and retailers can also lead to overproduction.

Another reason for overproduction may be the management philosophy or framework of decision making. There are cases where even though the operation managers pretend to follow lean manufacturing principles, their behaviors are further from many of the lean principles. Managers may not practice minimum inventory as a livable policy. Such proceeding often becomes a habit as long there is some level of profitability and senior managers do not challenge the operations to run at their full potential. Another common behavior is that of managers' non belief in planning improvement with more precise estimates which is also a negation of the lean principle of continuous improvement.

In will not forget the very common cause of over production which is poor operating practices that lead to poor quality and low throughput with the following consequences:

a) Managers decide to enlarge safety stocks of finished goods.

b) Managers quarantine defective products and then have to produce good parts following containment actions. In this case quarantined parts drive over production because managers must avoid starving their customers of products.

5.2.4) Consequences of overproduction waste

The consequences of overproduction are well known. Typically in a medium and long run, overproduction leads to inventories in house, at the retailers, or in distribution centers, creating inventory waste in the three locations. When unplanned customers do not purchase the inventories, managers have to apply rebates or sales. Rebates and sales erode profit margins, which lead to lower or negative cash flow. For products such as automobiles or motorcycles, rebates and sales drive lower resale values, and in some cases a sizable decrease in the perceive values of the brands.

Overproduction leads to extra cost of non value adding activities, which is the difference between products sold as ordered and product sold at rebate added to the cost of manpower overtime work premium if employees work overtime to produce extra products. For many companies in the USA there is often an overtime premium of 50% of the cost of direct labor. I will not forget to add the cost of holding inventory in yards or in warehouses which includes manpower, some insurance costs, and real estate costs.

An unintended consequence of overproduction is poor quality. When managers prioritize volumes over production, they often do not give any other choice to their subordinates but to mostly contain quality issues instead of solving them to the root cause. Again, the workforce pushed by managers violate the lean principle of taking the time to fix issues which results into excess scraps, excessive manpower costs with more employees than needed according to customer demand, and use of incentives to drive sales of products which quality is probably not the best in class.

5.2.5) Solutions to overproduction waste

A pull system helps avoid overproduction. However a complete pull system may not always be possible. In the case of consumers good sold in retail stores, the retailer uses analytics and forecasts the quantity of products to be ordered. The manufacturer receives orders under a pull system in such a case. If the forecast is not accurate, the retailer sells products on sales after the period allocated for selling the products. Just in time with minimum safety stock, excellent voice of the customer meaning clear understanding of customer wants, excellent production planning, effective communication among retailers, distributors, sales, and production planners will minimize overproduction.

A culture of continuous improvement with results in product quality and product delivery helps the manufacturer operation avoid firefighting, thus avoiding the temptation of overproduction in cases of a higher rate of defects and rework. When overproduction has become chronic, senior managers need to step up and initiate a cycle of improvement in the whole operation using for instance the plan do check act cycle (PDCA), team problem solving, employee empowerment, brainstorming of new ideas, and "Go See" also called Genchi Genbutsu

5.2.6) Exercises on overproduction waste

Group or individual exercise on overproduction waste 1
You have been in a store and found shoes on sale.

Q1.1) Draw a flow chart that illustrates the flow of shoes from the manufacturing facility to the retailer

Q1.2) Why would a shoe retailer place shoes on sale?

Q1.3) Is there waste for the retailer when shoes are sold on sale?

Q1.4) Is this a case of overproduction waste for the retailer if the retailer owns the manufacturing organization?

Q1.5) Is this a case of overproduction waste if the retailer is the customer and the manufacturing organization an outside supplier?

Group or individual exercise on overproduction waste 2
A bakery makes the same volume of French bread from Monday to Friday of every week; about 1600 lb of bread per day. On Saturday and Sunday the volume goes up by 30 percent. There has been a decline in sales from Monday to Wednesday for the last four weeks. The average daily sales for the first three days of the last four weeks were: week 1: 1520 lbs, week2: 1340 lb, week 3 1620 lbs, and for the current week 4: 1316 lbs. On week 3, the school district of the area was on fall break. On week 4, children went back to school again.

Q2.1) Advise the bakery manager on how to adjust production to minimize overproduction waste.

Q2.2) What adjustments to the bakery standard procedures need to be made to prevent similar issues?

Group or individual exercise on overproduction waste 3

Q3.1) Present an over production waste that occurred at one of your group member's work location.

Q3.2) What drove overproduction?

Q3.3) Who was involved in solving the issue?

Q3.4) Was reoccurrence prevented?

5.2.7) Case on overproduction waste

An automobile manufacturer with only one assembly plant in the U.S. had entered the U.S. market a year and half ago. The U.S. plant produces three vehicles, a sedan Sa, which is a very small vehicle of class A and a larger sedan, Sc which is also a compact vehicle of class C. The third vehicle is a crossover built on the same platform as Sc; it is called Cc. The sales of the three vehicles have increased sizably so that the plant is running on two shifts of 10 hours for four days in a row per week. The daily production rate of all three vehicles is 800 per day or 400 vehicles per shift, under a pull system. The production rate per type of vehicle has been 25% for vehicle Sa, 50% for vehicle Sc, and 25% for vehicle Cc. The CEO mandates the chief marketing executive (who also oversees sales) to increase incentives for all three vehicles in order to obtain an increase in sales volumes of 25% so the car maker can break even and be sizably profitable in the USA. He (the CEO) claims he is convinced that the incentives will give the results expected based on inputs given by a consultant. He expects the plant to run for the next few months for 10 hours per shift, five days per week in a row. You are regional managers working under the chief marketing officer. You need to help the chief marketing executive make a reasonable counter offer to the CEO.

Q1) Write the process steps of the flow of vehicles from the assembly process through the dealership finally to the end customer. Consider that all vehicles sold in this case have a customer for sure.

Q2) Write the process steps of the same flow when production runs for five days per week, 10 hours per day. Illustrate the storage of vehicles that do not have a customer for sure. Note: the only demand that is sure from customers is 800 vehicles per day, four days per week. Consider 200 days of production per year when running four days per week and 250 days of production when running five days per week

Q3) Complete a pro and con analysis for the strategy proposed by the CEO and for the current strategy (with 4 days of production per week).

Q4) complete a risk analysis in term of dollars in labor cost and profit. Consider an average cost of $30 per hour, and direct 400 assembly employees per shift. Consider a profit margin of $1500, $2000, and $3500 per respective vehicle Sa, Sc, and Cc when the vehicle is sold for sure before being assembled. Hint: Extra labor hours on Friday get paid at a premium of 50% which should negatively affect profit margins.

Q5) What is the value that could be wasted? Note: for the CEO's option, the manufacturer pays incentives of $1000 or $2000 with these responses: For a $1000 rebates, 50% vehicles are sold within four months and for $2000 rebate, 100% of extra vehicles are sold within four months. Dealers decline to carry any vehicle that may stands in a dealership for more than four months.

Q6) As the marketing executive, what would you advise the CEO to do?

5.3) Over processing waste

5.3.1) Definition
Over processing waste is waste that is generated either by adding more value than the customer expects or by producing beyond the required specifications. Redundant processes such as too many fasteners, over inspections, over handling, over-specifications; or washing clothes in a laundromat twice when once would have been enough are a few examples

5.3.2) Examples of over processing waste

Examples a)
An automobile manufacturer sets gap specification between the trunk door and the truck opening. If the specified gap is too tight with respect to customers' wants, the stamping operation works with specifications that are excessively tight, therefore more costly in term of control.

Examples b)
In a vehicle interior there is a class A surface of a plastic panel on an area not seen by the customer. A class A plastic surface is painted surface which is smooth, refined, and has an appealing appearance and that a vehicle occupant must see when he or she enters the vehicle.

Example c)
Having two different speedometers on a vehicle dashboard, one for Canada, in both mile per hour (mph) and in Kilometer per hour (kph) the other for the USA in mph while the Canada speedometer would have been enough. Here there is an unnecessary extra design.

5.3.3) Causes of over processing waste
Poor voice of the customers in product design and manufacturing process design, and processing error may lead to over processing. When designing products or service, the design team must capture the customers' wants and translate them into engineering design specification and manufacturing specifications. A lean design team would review redundancy which is wanted for product reliability versus redundancy which is excessive. The process design and the manufacturing design team must also agree on the process parameters to avoid giving the customers at a cost more than what they expect. The design should review overdesign with such activities as the improvement of the commonality of components.

Over processing may also be a result of a mistake and in such case the waste is also a waste of poor quality. Adding an in-process control device such as a Poka Yoke may help. Timers for processes that have time as a parameter and to control temperature are a few examples. You have probably experienced a steak too much done in a restaurant it is an example of over processing. It is over processing for the restaurant. The restaurant probably needs to time its oven or stove and retrain its cooks and waiters.

Other causes of chronic over processing may be the lack of management support for problem solving. The absence of regular audits, poor communication between design and production and a less than thorough control plans may lead to chronic over processing.

5.3.4) Consequences of over processing waste

Over processing waste leads to high processing costs. The extra processing cost includes extra labor cost when over processing in house. In a company designs a product to be outsourcing to a supplier, then the extra processing at the supplier manufacturing location will be included in the piece of the component or material being outsourced. Over processing in design may lead redundant components such as fasteners and in that case the cost of purchasing the extra component for the duration of the program is the cost of over processing. When over processing in offices or in manufacturing, the over processing cost is the total cost of extra processing which includes manpower costs, tooling cost, and energy cost. Extra costs drive profitability and cash flow differentials down. When over processing is a consequence of a process error, over processing leads to scrap costs, rework cost, and warranty costs.

5.3.5) Solutions to over processing waste

When design new products and news process the people involved need training in over processing waste identification. Engineers need to understand when redundancy becomes excessive. When specifications go beyond government regulation, engineers should be able to access if such over design is necessary, a company may use such overdesign markets safe products and attract more customers, in such cases marketing and engineering need to verify the profitability of such redesign.

Problem solving and in-process control may resolve over processing resulting from process mistake or error. Quality audits and an effective continuous improvement process may help avoid reoccurrence. When processing in offices the problem may go unnoticed but managers need find when there are excessive reviews of office products such as documents. The reviews become excessive ass son as their responses reach a state of diminishing returns. For instances if a customer submits documents for a mortgage application, and the document goes through many reviews, managers should know when to stop reviewing

Employees should use value stream mapping to identify non value adding activities of type reprocessing. Training the workforce in lean enterprise or in Six Sigma and empowering the workforce to identify and resolve occurrences of over processing may be an effective solution. Employees may receive such training only if senior managers support the waste elimination effort.

5.3.6) Exercises on over processing waste

Group or individual exercise on over processing waste 1

A class A surface is a painted surface which finish is refined with an appealing appearance and which is seen by the customer who enters a vehicle A while a class B surface is generally not seen by the customer and is less refined and less costly compared to a class A surface. A vehicle interior has a class A plastic panel surface on an area not seen by the customer while the surface should have been of class B. You are the product development engineer who finds about this opportunity. Note: There is over processing waste here.

Q1.1) As a team, describe how you would address this issue. List all the solutions that your group members propose.

Q1.2) Assuming the difference in prices between a class A surface and a class B surface is $0.05 per panel and that there are two panels per vehicle, if 500, 0000 vehicles are sold per year, what is the cost of this waste per year? What is the cost over 5 years (which is the duration of the program)?

Group or individual exercise on over processing waste 2

Some common examples of over processing waste are the following: Addition of chemicals where the amount of chemical has to be controlled to ensure a defined specification; and drying or cooling processes where both temperature and time have to be controlled to ensure a given material property.

Select a material or product that goes through one of the processes described above. Hints: Heat treatment, baking of food, mixing and cooling of drugs, heating of plastic material, addition of chemicals to drugs, addition of fillers to plastics.

Q2.1) Discuss among your team members what drive this kind of over processing the most?

Man, Machine, Measurement, material, process, environment?

Group or individual exercise on over processing waste 3

Think about your work. Please identify over processing waste that you may know of. Select one example given by one of your group members.

Q3.1) Describe the waste in question

Q3.2) What drove over processing?

Q3.3) Who was or should be involved in solving the issue?

Q3.4) Was reoccurrence prevented? How would you prevent reoccurrence?

5.4) Inventory waste

5.4.1) Definition

Inventory waste is waste that is a result of the storage of excess raw materials, components, or work in process, or finished products without adding value into it.

5.4.2) Examples of inventory waste

Example a)

The engineering level of raw material received in a factory changes as a result of new customer requirement. The inventory of material is no longer needed.

Example b)

A coffee shop purchases fresh milk for mixing in customers' orders of coffee or chocolate milk. The milk expires per specifications that figure on the label. Many bottles of milk are therefore wasted.

5.4.3) Causes of Inventory Waste

Work-in-process inventories and finished goods inventories cover unnecessary space, and increase the risk of damages, customer defects, and sale rebates. The absence of an effective pull system leads to inventory in house, in warehouse, and in retail centers. Quality defects may also lead to inventory when managers quarantine products that are suspicious of having defect. To cover for the shortage, managers let workers produce more products and ship them to customers. Here the presence of inventory of products suspected of quality defects is often a consequence of failure to stop to fix problems. The absence of effective team problem solving such as Six Sigma, five Whys, Shainin's problem solving, or 8D analysis; non effectiveness or non existence of Go See, Kaizen, and teamwork as drivers of continuous improvement lead to the existence of rework stations that become business as usual. If managers do not set objectives for minimum rework, inventory from poor quality will not decrease.

Poor planning as already described earlier when I discussed the causes and determinants of overproduction waste is another driver of inventory waste. Managers may not have analytic capabilities that allow them to plan production. Not believing in just in times (JIT) may also cause high inventory mostly for businesses that manufacture products to be sold to the customers. Poor planning may also lead to inventory from products or components purchased from a supplier. If a manufacturers order too many components from a supplier without matching the quantity to customers' demand then there will be inventories of components purchased from a supplier.

5.4.4) Consequences of Inventory Waste

Inventories generate high inventory cost when stored in a facility that requires maintenance, energy, security to protect inventories. Inventories of finished products also lead to rebates and ultimately to a lower brand equity. Because inventory waste drives rebates and other incentives, revenues per unit of product go down and in a long run, unit profit margin decreases.

The presence of inventories in manufacturing operations is usually positively correlated to either an ineffective control of quality, the presence of repair or rework workstations, or a pull system causing overproduction. As long as there is no stretched objective to decrease inventories and quantity of rework per shift, it will be difficult to improve first time throughput and quality. Presence of significant inventory waste encourages a state of ineffective problem solving with revolving containment actions becoming a testimony of daily firefighting.

5.4.5) Solutions to Inventory waste

Training managers and their subordinates in just-in-time increase the probability of having the workforce implement just-in-time effectively. Just-in-time (JIT) as a planning and delivery system will help eliminate inventory waste. However without the support of senior leaders, the manufacturing operation will not adopt just in time. JIT cannot be effective if the controls of quality and delivery are not effective.

When delivery is not effective, which is the case when throughput is low because of significant downtimes, then the risk that the manufacturer starves its customer becomes higher, meaning JIT becomes ineffective. Seemingly poor quality may cause the quarantine of quantities of products leading to low delivery. If the manufacturer does not quarantine and sort products that are suspect of poor quality then poor quality products reach customers and JIT is no longer effective. JIT means the delivery of good quality product on time. When business customers such as retailers or other manufacturing companies receive poor quality products, they may quarantine and ask the supplier to send them good units, they may sort at the cost of the supplier and make the supplier responsible for an eventual starvation of the customer. The point here is that poor quality drive inventory waste.

Manufacturers need to improve both quality and delivery, thus all the solutions that I listed for rework and quality defect waste, for overproduction waste, and for delay waste are also solutions to inventory waste. The solutions include at least effective pull system and Total Productive Maintenance (TPM). Team problem solving with methods such as 8D, Five Whys, Six Sigma, Go See (Genchi Genbutsu) where the problem occurs, and cycles of continuous improvement plan do check act all ensure a higher level of equipment availability and positively contribute to a higher quality level leading to fewer products in repair workstations.

5.4.6) Exercises on inventory waste

Group or individual exercise on inventory waste 1
You have been in a store and found clothes on sale.
Q1.1) Draw a flow chart for the flow of clothes from the manufacturer to the retailer
Q1.2) Is there a waste for the retailer when clothes are sold on sale?
Q1.3) Is this a case of inventory waste for the retailer if the retailer owns the manufacturing organization?
Q1.4) Is this a case of inventory waste if the retailer is the customer and the manufacturing organization is an outside supplier?
Q1.5) What would the retailer's managers do if all the clothes that are on sale are not sold?

Group or individual exercise on inventory waste 2
Think about your work. Please identify inventory waste that you may know of. Select one example given by one of your group members.
Q2.1) Describe the waste in question
Q2.2) What drove inventory build up?
Q2.3) Who was involved in solving the issue?
Q2.4) Was reoccurrence prevented?
Q2.5) Draw a process flow for the process in question
Q2.6) Give suggestions of improvement that should help eliminate the inventory waste identified.
Q2.7) How often do managers review inventory in your organization? Once per week?, once per month?

5.4.7) Case on inventory waste
A corporation that owns 10 hospitals uses nutritional solutions for its patients. The solutions have an expiration date of 12 months after they are manufactured. They

also have to be kept refrigerated at 40 degree F. A hospital uses an average of 300 solutions per day, or 1,095, 000 solutions per year, or 91250 solutions per month. The usages of solutions vary per hospital from 100 to 450. Hospitals are located in four different neighboring states in the Midwest of the USA.

The corporation signs a contract with a clause to order at least 1000, 000 solutions per year. Each solution cost $ 25 when purchased at a volume above 1000, 0000 and $27 when less than 1000,000 are purchased. The contract has to be signed before the beginning of each calendar year.

Q1) If the corporation purchases 990,000 solutions in a given year what does it lose or gain if it did not sign the 1000,000 minimum units purchased clause?

Q2) What is the minimum percentage of decrease in sale (number of units per year) that will justify not signing the clause?

Q3) What would happen if purchasing decides to purchase exactly the same number of solutions for each hospital?

Q4) Define a strategy to order solutions for each hospital with one objective (among others) being to have minimum inventory at the end of each month.

In the strategy above include how you will estimate future order of solutions.

Q5) If the corporation adds one more hospital, what will happen in term of overall order of solutions and confidence to the customer demand of solutions?

5.5) Quality defect and rework waste

8.5.1) Definition of defect and rework waste driven by manufacturing or services

Quality defect and Rework waste driven by manufacturing is waste that is a result of quality defects or rework caused by a variation on the manufacturing or service process. Variations can results from a human mistake, degradation or an error of manufacturing equipment, a defective component from a supplier, a damage or degradation through transportation, or staging in a warehouse or in yard

5. 5.2) Example of rework and defect waste driven by manufacturing or services

Example a)
A manufacturer of desktop computers recalls computers because the power units fail to function as a result of brittle wire snapping head that become broken overtime, a result of a second tier supplier defect.

Example b)
An automobile manufacturer recalls vehicles because of a risk of front brakes that prematurely fail. Products in the two quality recalls have to be repaired which is waste.

Example c)
A manufacturer of DVD players has to rework some of its DVDs because inspectors detect failures of the power control unit on some DVD players.

Example d)

An airline passenger arrives to Chicago coming from Africa. He checks his luggage but they are missing. The airline agrees to look for the luggage, and in case they find them, to send them to the passenger at his address in Michigan.

5.5.3) Causes of rework and defect waste driven by manufacturing or services

A non robust or non followed production control plan, non trained workers, no effective visual factory, no mistake proofing devices, poorly designed workspaces; poor designed processes may cause rework, scraps, and quality defects. When designing manufacturing processes and manufacturing operation, process designers may fail to ensure in-process quality control at the workstation.

5.5.4) Consequences of defect and rework waste driven by manufacturing or services

Quality defects driven by manufacturing may lead to poor customer satisfaction added to warranty repairs and even quality recalls. A customer may go to a competitor for their next purchase. If a vehicle's brake and disk brake assembly becomes loose, it is a manufacturing defect that generates a warranty repair and may generate a recall. Warranty occurrences are costly and recalls are costlier, thus defect wastes negatively affect the profitability and the positive differential cash flows of the enterprise.

Rework wastes in the manufacturing operation lead to higher production costs and to a more significant level of inventory staging inside or around the manufacturing facility. Rework wastes increases inventory costs and lead to rework costs which are wastes, and which all contribute to higher production costs. The occurrence of defect wastes and rework wastes negatively affect the brands of the enterprise.

As customers become subjects to quality recalls or warranty occurrences, many of the customers switch to competitors, decide not to refer the product to other potential customers, or tell stories about their warranty occurrences. As more people become aware of the poor quality of the brand, the value of the brand diminishes

5.5.5) Solutions to defects and rework waste that is driven by manufacturing or service

Jobs have to be ergonomically friendly, thus as process employees design jobs they need to minimize waste by making sure that the person doing the job often called the operator is in his or her natural workspaces. Being in the operator natural workspaces means the operator do not have to excessively walk, excessively stretch, twist, or bend. The operator should also be able to have enough light around the workspaces and should be able to feel comfortable with bearable temperature and air free of dust. Clear light and clean air enable workers to read work instructions and visual aid better and to stay focused on the job. If one or more of the requirements that I just listed are not fulfilled then the probability of having defects at the workstation increases. The absence of lean control methods also leads to quality defects.

Poka Yoke are mistake proofing devices that make sure that the work-in-process leaves the workstation only when quality is good as prescribed in the work instruction and in control plan. A mechanical fixture may not allow the operator to assemble a brake pedal on the location assigned to the accelerator pedal, which is an example of a Poka Yoke. The line may stop until the assembly of the wheel to the axle reaches specified torque of for instance 100 Newton meter and an angle of 360 degrees; which is another example of a Poka Yoke. The idea here is to consider the next workstation as a customer and to require that no defect reaches the next customer. In other words, defects should not travel; if they cannot be automatically controlled by for instance limit switches, an optical beam reader, or an automated scanner, they have to be controlled using closed loop inspections by the operator doing the job and by the another operator working down the line.

The chained inspections here described are build in-quality checks that ensure in process quality control. Let us be clear, a human being is not a robot and may not repeat perfect verification one hundred percent of the time. However, even with a one percent to five percent rate of mistake, build in quality check improved quality by thousand of percentages when compared to inspections at the end of the line for lines with tens to hundreds of jobs. Operators need to understand the requirements for the jobs. Visual aids describing the critical to the jobs and the steps that define the best way of doing the jobs help minimize occurrences of defects that can be attributed to the operators

When equipment breakdowns occur frequently quality is negatively affected because the capability of manufacturing equipment decreases and operators get distracted upon breakdowns. Total Productive Maintenance (TPM) or preventive maintenance combined with both predictive maintenance and teamwork significantly improves equipment availability and capability. Team problem solving with methods such as 8D Five Whys, and Six Sigma, Go See (Genchi Genbutsu) where the problem occurs, and cycles of continuous improvement plan do check act also (PDCA) enable team of workers to control both quality and equipment availability and to continuously improve, enabling the operation to meet stretched objective of operational excellence.

5.5.6) Definition of defect and rework waste driven by design
Defect and rework waste driven by design is waste that is a result of a flaw in design that the design team did not prevent through design verification or manufacturing validation and that reach the manufacturing operation or the end customer.

5.5.7) Examples of defect and rework waste driven by design

Example 5.e)
A pharmacy recall a drug sold in the form of pills because its content causes dangerous side effects

Example 5.f)
An automobile manufacturer recalls vehicles because vehicles often stall after driving them for 5000 to 10000 miles. The design team found that the wrong battery was assigned to the vehicle.

Example 5.g)
A retailer recalls food mixers because most customers have brought them back. they stop working after no more than three months of usage.

Example 5.h)
A food retail store recalls a brand of canned fish because customers complained the food was just too salty

5.5.8) Causes of rework and defect waste driven by design

Non robust design, incomplete design verification, less than thorough design verification, incomplete manufacturing validation may lead to defects driven by design. Even the manufacturing operations is robust with no defect, a quality defect driven by design may arise within the manufacturing operation through testing or in services. Engineers may have failed to correctly translate customer wants into engineering specifications. When engineers fail to correctly perform design for manufacturing analyses, design for reliability analyses, sensitivity analysis, design failure modes and effects analyses then defect from design may occur throughout the manufacturing operation.

Engineers may also wrongly translate customers' wants into design specification in such cases the product or service may fail. Incorrect design verification may occurs when either prototypes are not representative of the final products, a test done is not fully representative of static efforts, dynamic efforts, exposure to service or usage environments such as high temperature, cold weather, snow, rain, or else. Testing equipment may have a failure not detected by test engineers in such case the test engineers approve the tests when they should have not. An engineering judgment also be flawed because a mistake in the computation of analytic formula, mistake in a formula, or wrong assumptions.

Assumptions for simulations may also not fully represent the customer experience or the engineers may interpret the results of the simulation wrongly. There are many opportunities for contributing to a flaw in a design. If only one engineer makes a decision at each stage of the design verification then the risk of flaw in a design increases. Seemingly when the design team and the manufacturing team validate the manufacturability of the design, the two teams should take time to test as much as possible the product made during manufacturing validation because by then the prototypes are closer to the final products to be sold to the customers.

Incorrect engineering analyses can lead to mistakes that even if small may have adverse consequences in service. Poor verification of tolerance stack-up, incomplete or wrong sensitivity analyses, may lead to defects driven by design. Poor ethic in testing of drug may also lead to defects driven by design. If through the plan do check act improvement cycles of design, participants in the cycle are afraid to raise their voice issues that may affect the quality of the product then major problems that may cause quality recalls may be overlooked.

5.5.9) Consequences of Defect and Rework Waste Driven By Design

Flaws in design may lead to poor customer satisfaction without warranty or recall. However in this case customer may go to a competitor for their next purchase. For instance an automobile manufacturer may announce on its owner manual that the fuel consumption of its vehicle is 24 miles per gallon in city and 27 miles per gallon on highways. Many customers purchase the vehicles. The customers find that after driving vehicles for about a year, the fuel consumption in cities is about 20 miles per gallon and of highway about 23 miles per gallons. The customers may not complaints but many of them will switch to different automobile manufacturers' brands in the next purchase. Manufacturers may not get referral from words of mouth, a significant driver of customer retention or new customer acquisition.

In many cases design defects may affect many more products than manufacturing defects because manufacturing defects often depend on temporary variations whereas design defects apply to all the products manufactured with a common design. When design defects affect safety regulated functions or features such seat belts or airbags that help save lives in cars, absence of lead on children toys, or absences of averse health side effect for drugs, they usually lead to recall that cost many millions of dollars to the manufacturer,

5.5.10) Solutions to defect and rework defect driven by design

To have an outstanding design quality, the engineering team needs to work rigorously using a system approach in design. Design verification from documentation of design failure effects analyses, through design verification plan and reports, compatibility verification at the interfaces, testing, and simulations have to be rigorous with eyes reviewing the same item at each stage of design verification. For instance a manufacturing engineer, a design engineer, a quality engineer, a material expert, and a test engineer should all verify the results of given tests. Doing so bring consensus in engineering decision making and minimize the risk of wrong decisions.

Toyota uses the A3 form that a program engineer passes to experts of different functions so they can assign their signatures on the form testifying that they agree with the design decision. At first such process may appear slow but for a product or service program it is a process that shortens product development time because it minimizes the risk of engineering changes downstream. Cross-functional teams should also complete failure mode effects analyses. It is the responsibility of the manufacturer's design team to make sure that FMEAs are completed rigorously in house or at the supplier location. The ratings that FMEA team members assign into the FMEA form have to represent reality.

The design team needs to also follow lean principles that affect quality. Problems should be reviewed at Gemba (the place). A chief engineer and a few program team members may spend some time with customers to live their experiences. In the automobile industry engineers may drive vehicles similar to the one to be designed to feel the driving experience and foresee what needs to be improved upon. The design team may have reviews in test areas or at the supplier design location in order to better understand the design.

Engineering managers need to remove tasks that do not add value and that are unnecessary from the engineers' lists of tasks. For instance there should be an upper limit on the time allocated for meetings so that the engineering spend most of their time doing design work. To drive continuous improvement, there should be a list of lesson learned from each program that can be replicated in other programs, which speed up the time to reach flawless execution of design. Managers need to allocate fund for training and train engineers in techniques that ensure robust design such as design for Six Sigma and design for manufacturing.

5.5.11) Group Exercise on Rework and Defect Waste

Group exercise on rework and defect waste 1

An airline passenger arrives to Chicago coming from Africa. He checks his luggage on the luggage area but they are missing. The airline agrees to look for the luggage, and in case they find them, to send them to the passenger at his address in

Michigan. The airline in question called Worldwide Airline had had many of those incidents in the past. Many customers have complained. Customers have even started talking, spreading world of mouth about their unfortunate experience. Working as customer service managerial team members, responsible for improving customer satisfaction you need to resolve this issue.

Q1.1) Define the steps of the flow of luggage from the embarked airport to the destination airport, for a straight flight without stop. Identify areas with opportunities for the luggage to be set off the normal flow to final destination (where the defect mechanism occurs).

Q1.2) Define the steps of the flow of luggage from the embarked airport to the destination airport, assuming, there is a stop on a transit airport which is Zurich, Switzerland, where the passenger embarks to a new airplane. Identify areas with opportunities or luggage to be set off the normal flow to final destination.

Q1.3) For the trip with a transit stop, identify opportunities of improvements (actions that would prevent mistakes to occur). Those actions should eliminate missing or wrong luggage.

Q1.4) What steps would you take to prevent reoccurrence of these customer complaints?

Group exercise on rework and defect waste 2
Think about your work. Identify rework and defect waste that you have experienced at your place of work. Select one example given by one of your group members.

Q2.1) Describe the waste in question
Q2.2) What drove reworks and defect wastes?
Q2.3) Who was involved in solving the issue?
Q2.4) Was reoccurrence prevented?

Group exercise on rework and defect waste 3
A computer manufacturer starts selling its first product which is a foldable laptop computer with a screen and the hard drive unit in two units joined at the edges like most laptop made from the 2000s years through the first half of the 2010s
. After using the computer for a few months the junction between the screen and the hard drive unit breaks for many using, a proof for most users that the material at the junction is not strong enough

Q3.1) What type of waste is this defect waste: Driven by manufacturing or by design? State your reason.

Q3.2) What should the manufacturer do?

Q3.3) How can the manufacturer test new prototypes or new computer newly made computers to detect this defects

Q3.4). Assuming a new laptop computer costs 250 US dollars, and that the manufacturer would have to fix 55% of the computers sold, estimate the cost of repairs. The number of computers that are already in the pipeline is 100600. You must estimate the manpower cost and the material cost for repair.

5.5.12) Case on rework and defect waste

47

An automobile manufacturer recalls vehicles because of a risk of front brakes that prematurely fail. Products in those two recalls have to be repaired, which is waste.

The manufacturer assembly plant receives rotors already assembled with brake calipers from a supplier located 150 miles from the assembly operation. The rotors and brake sub-assemblies are assembled to the rear and front axles on an axle line that is set adjacent to the beginning of the final line feeding into it just before the engine decking operation

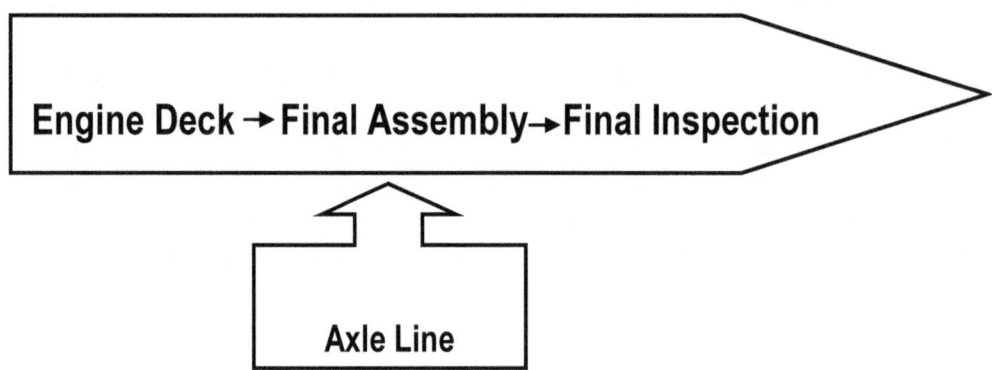

Figure 7. A View of the Manufacturing Operation

Brake quality issues can probably cause recalls, more customers can be injured. At this point, there has been no injury. You are the quality manager of the vehicle operation here discussed. You need to protect both customers and your company. Based on reviews of repairs performed at dealerships, you should assume here that there are four potential sources of brake customer defects: loose caliper, leakages, wrong calipers, and cables mis-assembled. Your plant manager just received two emails, one from the VP of quality, and the other from the VP of manufacturing. Both are aware of the three occurrences found at dealerships. They have reminded the plant manager that the company cannot afford a recall and solving the current brake defects was a company top priority.

The plant vehicle engineering manager has gathered the following data to help the team

Table 3
List of Quality Defects

Defects or complaints	Counts	Where detected	Comments
Premature brake failure	3	Customer in service	Need more information
Brake fluid leakage	26	Final assembly line	Loose assembly axle line
Wrong caliper	4	Final assembly line	From the supplier
brake cable mis-assembled	1	Final assembly line	From the supplier

Q.1) What is the first thing that you should do?
Q.2) Draw a process flow diagram of the rotor and caliper assembly work-in-process from the supplier to the final inspection; such a process must have inspection steps that will minimize occurrences of these defects.
Q.3) How can this defect be completely prevented. Hint: Build in quality checks, locking mechanism, automatic controls, in process quality control, audits, PDCA, others.
Q.4) Who are the people that should be involved in resolving these issues.
Q.5) Present your findings

5.6) Delay waste

5.6.1) Definition
Delay waste is a waste that results from the non addition of value that occurs when an activity that should have added value stops waiting to be started usually because of either the non availability of resources, a variation in the process, a physical constraint, or a management decision.

5.6.2) Examples of delay waste

Example 6.a)
A break down on an automobile final assembly line causes upstream assembly lines to progressively become idle until all the assembly lines are idle.

Example 6.b)
A robot breaks down many times in a manufacturing operation, and adjacent workers have to wait for the repairmen to come.

Example 6.c)
A business man files for a business license. The license should be complete in three business days but the business man waits for two full weeks without answer.

Example 6.d)
A bank hires three tellers but they often spend up to 15 minutes without a customer every hour.

Example 6.e)
A supplier misses its shipment. The customer manufacturing plant waits for the supply of parts, which causes a delay of two days of production. The manufacturer subsequently misses to supply the final products to the end customers on time.

5.6.3) Causes of delay waste
Poor maintenance of equipment without effective problem solving or effective maintenance management such as total productive maintenance (TPM) will cause equipment downtimes driving operators to be idle. Quality defects lead to equipment or production line downtimes. Poor material planning, poor supplier quality, and ineffective supplier delivery also lead to downtimes as a result of starvation of parts.

Poor production system analyses and design, simulation not used in production design, and poor or non effective problem solving will also lead to production line or production equipment downtimes. In case of starvation of parts or equipment downtimes that is too long, an assembly line will be blocked downstream or starved of work-in-process upstream. Chronic downtime is often a result of absence of continuous improvement that I have already discussed earlier for quality defects and rework waste.

In service or office businesses, delay waste may be the result of several managerial decisions, process factors, or structural factors. An employee may be absent increasing process times because fewer employees have to do more work causing delays. Process errors or mistakes may cause reprocessing leading to starvation of work for other workers assigned to some process steps. Mistakes may be a result of poor training. In project management mistakes, poor work, and poor planning cause delays. In a restaurant, when customers wait for food too long there is delay waste.

As long as managers of a service organization do not consider delay waste as a cause poor service performance and resolve it, delay waste will be chronic. The absence of planned customer feedback needed to take improvement actions and the ignorance of customer feedback by management help maintain poor service delivery. Management ignoring frameworks such as lean enterprise or Six Sigma may not help resolve delay waste in services. For network driven services such as airlines poor planning combines with poor training and poor process design lead to delay waste. Factors independent from management such as bad weather and accidents may also cause delay wastes in various services that depend on the transportation of people or goods. There is also delay waste in product development.

In most companies that design products and services, the goal is to shorten product development time, which decreases product development cost and makes the enterprise more competitive. Many of the factors that I already discussed for services may cause delay waste in product development. Poor training, poor work, poor coordination, and poor planning in general cause delays in product development. If engineers spends more time in meetings, they will spend shorter times designing products then delaying expected work downstream such as testing, simulation, or engineering reviews. A poor estimate of the time needed to accomplish previous work will cause management to delay a previously scheduled review in a later time which is waste. If suppliers of prototypes are not efficient enough, engineers will not receive prototypes on time which will delay their planned work with prototypes. As long as management does not take the decision to continuously improve product development processes, there will be delay waste in product development.

5.6.4) Consequences of delay waste

Delay wastes cause low throughput, low delivery, higher labor cost, and even poor quality in manufacturing, services, and product development. In manufacturing, because delay waste increases lead times the cost per unit increases negatively affecting profitability. Poor quality from operators as a result of the absence of work is another consequence of delay waste. In an assembly line when operators stop working for a long time, they become more likely to make mistakes because the stoppage of the line made them lose the natural cadence of work. Operators may temporally lose their focus when the line starts again.

For services, delay wastes lead to lower customer satisfaction and fewer

50

customers, causing lower revenues. In product development, when a meeting is cancelled late, the employees who have planned for the meeting have to adjust and depending on the time of the day, they may lose their cadence of doing a good job. What is sure in this very few employees appreciate late notices on cancelled meetings which may negatively affect their morale. Delay waste negatively affects the bottom line of the organization either in manufacturing, product development, or services. For automobile suppliers, starving a vehicle operation of parts makes the manufacturing loose profit margins and the supplier has to cover for such losses.

5.6.5) Solutions to delay waste

The design of the facility has to be robust enough to account for all the links among different productions. Facility planners need to identify the weakest links which determine the throughput of the manufacturing operation. Facility planners need to also account for buffers where it is necessary to minimize delays that are the result of the physical design or the dynamic of the production line. Managers need to also improve delivery

To improve delivery managers should have their workforce use total productive maintenance (TPM) or a combination of predictive maintenance, preventive maintenance, and lean tools. Besides, managers must use team problem solving with methods such as 8D Five Whys, and Six Sigma, quick change over (SMED), Go See (Genchi Genbutsu) where the problem occurs, and cycles of continuous improvement plan do check act (PDCA), thus ensuring a higher level of equipment availability and a higher quality level.

Because by improving quality, managers will reduce line downtimes, which will reduce delays, all the solutions that I have described for defect waste driven by manufacturing enable the minimization of delay waste. Kanban, good warehouse management which includes a layout of part locations and training of material delivery workers, good maintenance of fork lift trucks and tow trucks, and training enable the minimization of starvation of parts. The role of the supplier quality assistance department is critical to ensure that suppliers deliver good parts on time. Audits at the supplier manufacturing location and joint problem solving enable the supplier to improve its quality and delivery which minimizes the risking of starving the manufacturer of component.

5.6.6) Group or individual exercises on delay waste

Group or individual exercise delay waste 1

A break down on an automobile final assembly line causes upstream assembly lines to progressively become idle until all the assembly lines are idle. This kind of issue has been repetitive. Working as team, please complete the following:

Q1.1) List all potential causes of this kind of issues. Hint: An assembly line can be down or lose its speed. It can be down with micro stops and longer breakdowns. Think about a fishbone diagram. Man, machine, material, measurement, process, and environment.

Q1.2) How would you solve this issue?

Q1.3) Whom should you involve for solving this issue?

Q1.4) Which process would you follow to have the assembly line flowing as expected every day?

Group or individual exercise delay waste 2

A chain of grocery store has experienced delay s in the delivery of its most popular brand of peanut butter.

Q2.1) What is the waste for the chain of grocery?

Q2.2) If the manufacturer penalizes the supplier every time the supplier misses a delivery what is the waste for the supplier? What are other negative consequences?

Q2.3) How can the grocery store help resolve this issue? Why should it do so?

Group or individual exercise delay waste 3

Think about your work. Please identify a delay waste that you have experienced at your place of work. Select one example given by one of your group members.

Q3.1) Describe the waste in question

Q3.2) What drove delay waste?

Q3.3) Who was involved in solving the issue?

Q3.4) Was reoccurrence prevented?

5.6.7) Case on delay waste

Tom Wilson, a businessman had just filed for a business license. The license should be complete in three business days but the business man waits for two full months without answer. In this office of the ministry of industries of a developing country, corruption has been known to be a problem for business practice. The business man has told his story to friends, relatives, and officials. A few days ago, he was in a bar with a few acquaintances and told them about his misfortunes. They all started laughing. They explained to him that he had to give a bribe to the official who was handling his business license file. He had heard the same advice from most people that he spoke to. Tom Wilson was trained in business in the USA. He believes in ethics and even his business training emphasized the need for ethics in business.

Q1) Tom Wilson approaches you for advice. What would you advise him to do? What are the consequences for this delay waste for

Q2) Tom Wilson as a businessman?

Q3) For the whole developing country?

Q4) Assuming you are in the Tom Wilson's shoes. You are a U.S. businessman who comes up to this situation in Africa. As a U.S. resident or national, you cannot accept bribes because of the Foreign Corrupt Practices Act (FCPA) of 1977, what would you do?

Q5) What are the consequences of delays from corruption for the world economy?

5.7) Transportation waste

5.7.1) Definition

Transportation waste is a waste which is a result of an unnecessary movement of material or work-in-process. Such waste may occur in service, manufacturing, or service organizations.

5.7.2) Examples of transportation waste

Examples.7.a)

At the entrance of an emergency room, there are many vehicles waiting along the nearest drive way. When an ambulance arrives with patients, the ambulance has to stand 80 feet further from the entrance. The emergency personnel must transport the patient on a wheel bed while every second counts.

Example 7.b)

A material planner whose plant is very busy because of a high demand of its products is looking for three skids of components all over the plant floor. On that day, the regular fork lift truck driver calls in seek, and the replacement person is being trained. No one in the plant knows where the regular driver stored the critical components.

Example 7.c)

Because of a lack of capacity allocated to a given product, a manufacturing company can only produce half of the weekly required quantity of products. For that reason, it has to ship the weekly customer demand twice to minimize shortage at the customer location.

Example 7.d)

A package and mail delivery company has many drivers deliver packages in an allocated territory. If the routes followed by drivers are not optimized with minimum distance, then the extra miles beyond the minimum distances are transportation wastes.

5.7.3) Causes of transportation waste

Poor facility planning for new manufacturing operations or new service operations will cause the transportation of materials for unnecessarily long distances. When facility planners do not optimize the physical design of the facility they planned for there will be transportation waste in many forms such as longer lead times, higher energy costs, and higher transportation costs. If managers do not maintain conveyors or other transportation equipment at a higher level, then delay waste as downtime may add up to transportation waste.

Some of the transportation waste is necessary because it depends on the facility layout. In a vehicle assembly plant painted vehicle bodies from the paint shop have to be transported to the final areas for further assemblies to the body. Door panels have to be transported as well to the final areas for assembly. On another assembly plant when employees transport work-in-process from one manufacturing cell to the assembly line there is transportation waste.

In case process planners do not optimize each operation working space then larger parts may need sequencing. Workers may transport the large parts to a sequencing operation which is waste. An operator may bring parts on a tow truck to the assembly line. This is an example of operations designed with transportation waste in it. When process planning has not been trained in waste identification, there is a risk of designing such workstations in a manufacturing facility.

If we expand the scope of the operation to the global market, then the transport of components from a supplier to a manufacturer is necessary waste which can be sizable if a manufacturer from the USA receives components from a supplier facility set in another continent. Here again a poor supplier localization strategy will lead to higher transportation costs. In the manufacturing facility, there is waste in the transportation of components from the staging areas to the assembly line. Again poor warehouse planning may lead to higher transportation costs that could have been minimized.

5.7.4) Consequences of transportation waste
Transportation waste leads to high production costs in the form of manpower cost and energy cost and manpower cost which affect the bottom line. As stated earlier, transportation waste may also lead to delay when a transportation equipment breakdowns. Because transportation waste may increase manufacturing lead time, it negatively affects productivity. The waste should be minimized.

5.7.5) Solutions to transportation waste
Process designers and manufacturing layout planners should minimize transportation of work-in-process or transportation of components when they design a manufacturing operation and a job workstation. They may use value stream mapping, and optimization that relies son linear programming. Setting up suppliers around the manufacturing operation, a setup known as a supplier park, helps minimize supply transportation cost. Having the workforce trained in waste identification and in lean methods in general helps minimize the risk of setting up another workstation with significant transportation waste. To avoid adding more waste from transportation equipment breakdowns, the workforce needs to be well trained in preventive maintenance or total productive maintenance and apply the maintenance methods on transportation equipment such conveyors, forklift trucks, tow trucks, and vehicles.

5.7.6) Exercises on transportation waste

Group or individual exercise on transportation waste 1
At the entrance of an emergency room, there are many vehicles waiting along the nearest drive way. When an ambulance arrives with a patient arrives, the ambulance has to stand 80 feet further from the entrance. The emergency personnel then has to transport the patient on a wheel while every second counts
Q1.1) Describe the transportation waste here
Q1.2) What are the consequences of this waste for the customer and for the emergency care service?
Q1.3) How can you prevent this waste?

Group or individual exercise on transportation waste 2
A material planner working in a manufacturing facility that is busy because of a high demand of its products is looking for three skids of components all over the plant floor. On that day, the regular fork lift truck driver calls in seek, and the replacement person is being trained.
Q2.1) Describe the transportation waste here
Q2.2) What are the consequences of this waste for the customer and for the manufacturing company?
Q2.3) How can you prevent this waste?

Group or individual exercise on transportation waste 3

Think about your work. Please identify transportation waste that you have experienced at your place of work. Select one example given by one of your group members.

Q3.1) Describe the transportation waste in question

Q3.2) What drove transportation waste?

Q3.3) Who was involved in solving the issue?

Q3.4) Was reoccurrence prevented?

5.7.7) Case on transportation waste

Two years ago, a new company called New Motors Inc built a motorcycle assembly plant in the city of Wilberg. The company makes all the parts itself except for engines. For now it is outsourcing engines from Patterson Engines Inc, a supplier located in the City of Patterson 500 miles away from Wilberg. Last winter, because of the snow, the truck transporting engines arrived at least two days late twice and the plant lost five days of production. As a reminder, last year winter was not a harsh one and the plant may lose weeks of products in the advent of a harsh winter.

Management is thinking about minimizing the risk inherent to transportation as well as the transportation cost which savings even though not it the order of millions of US dollars still accounts for about $126000 per year. Management is thinking about two solutions:

Option 1

Have another small supplier open a small plant just for the manufacturing of New Motors's engines. The annual demand of motorcycle is 160000 motorcycles per year. The supplier will be able to have a labor cost 25% smaller than that of New Motors Inc. If option 1 is chosen, the small supplier will be called Advanced Engines LLC. The small supplier will be located one mile from the New Motors location. Transportation costs in this case will account for $50000 for two deliveries of many engines per week.

Option 2

Make engines in house. The cost of labor will be higher by 33% than that of Advanced Motors LLC since the labor cost of Advanced Motor LLC is 25% smaller than New Motors Inc. The only advantage for the manpower will be that of manpower with a greater capability to build quality products and better communication. New Motors Inc will have to invest 80000 dollars in capital equipment to set up a small line for engine assembly. There is enough space in the plant for the engine line.

Wilfred James, New Motors Inc's General Manager raised a concern of having in house complacency meaning that New Motors' managers may not make the in house engine team as accountable as they would make an external supplier accountable for poor quality and poor delivery. He also hinted another advantage of option 2 which was that of having more people in house to help in process improvement. On the second Monday of February, he called for meeting at 2:00 PM. The purpose of the meeting was to make a decision on one of the two options.

You are the Manufacturing Manager of New Motors Inc,

Q1) Enunciate and compute in US dollars the differential waste of ordering engines from Patterson Engines Inc versus ordering engines from Advanced Motor LLC. Patterson Engine Inc's piece price is $0.5 smaller than that of Advanced Motor LLC.

Q2) Enunciate and compute in US dollars the differential waste of ordering engines from Advanced Motor LLC versus manufacturing engines in house.

Q3) From the two exercises on 1) and 2), clarify the transportation waste (description and estimate of monetary amount or cost associated)

Q4) Propose a solution to Wilfred James. Consider tangibles benefits and intangible but qualitative benefits.

5.8) Poor utilization of resources waste

5.8.1) Definition of poor utilization of human capital waste

There is a waste of human capital when in an organization managers do not take into account diversity of employees, managers do not develop talents with equity ad objectivity, and managers do not optimize the use of intellectual capital to add value or the use of the capabilities of their workforce. Intellectual capital includes the overall knowledge of the enterprise. Knowledge can be tacit (not explicitly written but identifiable through common actions) or explicit. Human capital includes all the intangible resources of the individuals or groups of individuals within an organization that can help the organization be competitive. Examples of such resources are: knowledge, skills, habits, patents, experiences, judgment, and intelligence.

5.8.2) Examples of poor utilization of human capital waste

Example a)
An online university assigns 20 students to each classroom when an instructor can handle up to 40 students without affecting teaching quality.

Example b)
A given company must improve its performance. The company defines the change strategy and tactics top down with minimal consideration of the suggestions of employees who work on processes. In this case, there is a waste of tacit knowledge that could have led to greater improvement.

Example c)
In another company, a manager organizes design reviews for its products. In the meetings, only the manager and two other employees make decisions and give feedbacks. Suggestions given by some of their subordinates are ignored. Here there is also a waste of creativity and opportunities with diversity of options being limited.

Example d)
An executive decides to appoint his younger brother as the human resources manager, disregarding to objectively assess the capabilities of other internal and external candidates. Two years after the appointment, the morale in the company is low and many workers point out that the human resources department does not make people accountable.

Example e)

A medical device manufacturer has in its workforce shipping and receiving clerk who is a trained quality engineer with various experiences in quality and certification is Six Sigma Black Belt. The human resources manager is aware of the skills of the shipping clerk. The quality manager asks the human resource manager to hire a quality engineer who is a certified Six Sigma Black Belt. The Human resource manager spends two months interviewing different outside candidates but completely ignores the shipping clerk

5.8.3) Causes of poor utilization of human capital waste

Discrimination and the lack of objectivity in the selection, development, and selection of employees hurts the organization because the organization missing many opportunities leads to poor utilization of human resources waste as long as there is no lawsuit involved. If there is a lawsuit, waste which is a consequence of the lawsuit is non compliance to the organization code of conduct waste which I discuss further.

A poor human resources department that overlooks unfairness in people development, performance appraisal, and compensation is a catalyst for poor utilization of human resources. When the human resources manager does not work with functional managers to offer training on company code of conduct, people development, performance appraisal, diversity, and compensation then there will be variations in the promotion and development of employees. Job description without clear, realistic, and measurable objectives enable unfair appraisal of employees often at the discretion of the managers.

The human resources manager should be courageous enough to protect the interest of the organization without being afraid of the position power that some functional managers may have. However sometimes, human resources managers wrongly protects managers who do not follow the rules of equity, which does not help promote equal treatment of all employees. Poor communication of job requirement is another factor that may enable poor utilization of human resources waste. If managers do not lead by example and do not communicate the necessity of objectivity and transparence in the development and reward of employees, there will still be many occurrences of unfair reward and promotion of employees. Functional managers' decision making may also drive poor usage of knowledge

Managers may fail to plan for knowledge retention when employees retire or leave for new jobs allowing tacit knowledge to dissipate without being captured in written instructions or procedures Not having procedures and work instructions in digital files that are secure increases the risk of losing valuable knowledge. Managers may also fail to set up database and data mining for critical knowledge that the organizations may use for current or future operations and for developing new products and services. However some causes of poor utilization of human resources waste are cultural.

In a top down or command and control culture, there is a higher propensity to have managers promote people that they like instead of people who do a good job. In such a culture managers may also promote only people who believe in command and control. When compared to a flat organization, a stiff organization with many managerial levels enables a non objective promotion and a poor development of employees. One of the reasons is that because there are many managerial levels, many employees including managers are driven by eventual opportunities to move up the ladders, thus managers may end up promoting their self interests while spending little time and resources to develop employees

.

5.8.4) Consequences of poor utilization of human capital waste

With human capital waste, the enterprise misses many opportunities for positive contributions. Such contributions may add value without limit. The foundations of any lean enterprise or any learning organization rely on its people. If people are not involved in the lean enterprise processes, if management does not value their potential and reward their contribution, a lean enterprise may not survive with resilience and continuity and there will be no effective lean culture. By valuing employees' suggestions and creativity, an organization can minimize the other wastes here discussed. Minimizing waste of human and intellectual resources leads to the minimization of the other wastes. The enterprise will be missing many opportunities of improvement in operation deliverable and many opportunities to innovate. When managers do not select an employee who has more capabilities than employees that managers have promoted, there are two direct consequences.

First the organization receives poorer achievements for the work done in general, misses potential ideas that could have been breakthrough innovation or great opportunities for operational improvement, and the managers and the employees that they promoted just built a larger team of future managers who will more likely be subjective in their selection and promotion of employees. Such mechanism promotes the growth of a silo of employees whose self-interests come first before the interest of the organization even though managers involved state otherwise.

Second, the employee with greater capability who was not selected for a deserved promotion in many cases becomes a disgruntled employee whose performance may decline and who may leave the organization if given a similar or better opportunity outside of the organization. The monetary amounts of the wastes that I just described are difficult to fully appraise but can still be appraised overtime. They are examples of cultural traits that silently lead to a decline in the organization competitiveness.

Poor knowledge management also leads to missing opportunities for operational improvement, creativity, and innovation. When experienced employees leave for another employees ore retire if management did not capture their knowledge in written processes and by training other employees the companies loses valuable knowledge. Having many patents and not leveraging when there is an opportunity is waste of intellectual capital

Competitors that maximize the use of their human capital and the use of knowledge in general will have an edge in the development of products and services. Such competitors may have better returns over time compared to companies that have a significant waste of human capital. In a long run, companies that have waste of human capital will be less competitive compared to the competitors.

5.8.5) Solutions to poor utilization human resources waste

Because tacit knowledge may disappears when the people who carry it leave, it is necessary to carry most of it in the form of explicit knowledge. Training new employees when current employees leave or when employees retire is necessary in order to capture tacit and explicit knowledge. Hence planning for the retirement of employees is necessary and should not only involve the human resources manager and the functional managers. When current knowledgeable employees decide to leave for new jobs, it is necessary to ask them to stay a few weeks beyond the common two weeks of notice and use the time to capture as much knowledge as possible by training employees and by having the employees who leave organize knowledge data for use in the future by other employees.

Issuing patents for not only products but also for methods help capture knowledge that the organization may use to develop new products or services or to design processes that will be difficult for the competitors to imitate. Thus, managers need to make sure that the company has databases of knowledge and use data mining and analytics to generate valuable business insight that enable the organization to be competitive in a fluctuating market. However managers also need to develop behaviors that drive fairness in the development and promotion of employees.

A good human resource department helps set the tone by working with managers to offer training on company code of conduct, people development, performance appraisal, and compensation. The objectives and measurable for each should be clear and should figure in the job description. Functional managers need to make sure that employees understand their jobs, know the schedule of feedback, and know how to record their accomplishments. Senior managers need to lead by example and communicate the necessity of objectivity and transparence in the development and reward of employees. Audits and feedback in the form of surveys are necessary. Surveys should be anonymous and managers should not retaliate in case they found out the employees who more likely reported bad behaviors. Managers and supervisors need to be accountable for not following the rules of equity in the promotion and development of employees

5.8.6) Definition of non human capital resources waste

This is the waste led by the poor utilization of non human capital resources such as manufacturing equipment, other infrastructures, building, and facilities in manufacturing, services, government, and product development.

5.8.7) Examples of poor utilization of non human capital resource waste

Example f)

A car manufacturer designs a vehicle that is unnecessarily too heavy and consumes too much gas than it should have consumed had the manufacturers defined more stringent weight and fuel efficiency objectives. There is waste in natural resources because the company use too much steel in vehicles components is and gas used by drivers in service.

Example g)

A chemical company manufactures detergents loaded in plastic cardboard boxes. The company does not promote recycling of empty boxes to its customers, which leads to fewer consumers recycling their empty boxes. This is waste of raw material.

Example h)

An automobile manufacturer has a capacity utilization of 75%. In this case 25% of capacity is wasted.

5.8.8) Causes of poor utilization of non human capital resources waste

The absence of an effective pull system drives poor capacity utilization which is waste. At the start of the new operation managers need to make sure that they understand the customer wants and avoid an over estimate of initial capital investment. When initial capital investment is too large at start, it will become quite difficult for managers to scale it down in the future if future demands or products are below the initial estimates. In all cases poor maintenance will still lead to poor utilization of resources waste. For manufacturing equipment the waste may sometime be captured in term of delay waste or quality defect and rework wastes.

However the scope of lean enterprise is wider than just the direct manufacturing operation made of processes, manufacturing equipment, and people. Heaters, air conditioners, rest rooms, ovens in kitchen, water filter, forklift trucks, vehicles, cleaning equipment, computers, computer network, and databases all have to be maintained. Manager often pay less attention to non manufacturing equipment which may end up costing sizable amount of money because of poor maintenance. Poor maintenance of equipment leads to equipment downtime and frequent breakdowns. When managers fail to select a good framework for maintaining equipment they open the door to a system of repairs after breakdowns. Framework such as Total Productive Maintenance which relies on skills development, joined work between skill trades employees and production employees for basic maintenance tasks and continuous improvement in equipment maintainability help minimize equipment downtime.

When considering natural resources, if the organization does not have any environmental strategy, it will use natural resources without looking for solutions that may replace fossil fuels or fossil minerals. The absence of management support for recyclability or for using green power technologies are all determinants of poor use of non human capital resources. Except for the automobile industries, most industries do not have regulations that mandate the use of green technologies at a given rate of usage or to minimize emissions of either carbon or nitrogen. Most books on lean enterprise had not considered poor utilization of natural resources as waste by the end of year 2015.

5.8.9) Consequences of poor utilization of non human capital resources waste

Poor utilization of non human resources waste leads to increases in operating expenses and therefore negatively affects the organization bottom line. Poor utilization of information and technology resources can cause an organization to lose files that may be valuable assets. In the specific case of the automobile industry over capacity which is a poor utilization of plant and equipment hinder many manufacturers to either breakeven or reach higher level of added positive cash flows. Poor utilization of non human resources also negatively affects hygiene and safety. When people are not well trained in the use of heavy manufacturing equipment, injuries and even casualties may occur.

Poor maintenance of facility in services may be a deterrent to customers' purchases, hence giving the business a bad reputation. Poor utilization of natural resources affects the environment whether or not one believes in climate changes or not. The truth is that fossil resources are limited, thus all human beings should use them with care for future generations and must keep driving innovation that will eventually help create substitute materials that are synthetic.

5.8.10) Solutions to poor utilization of non human capital resources waste

Considering a pull system as a standard process before the purchase of new manufacturing equipment and planning for additional equipment later as demand increases help minimize overcapacity waste. Lean tools such as TPM, Kaizen, Genchi Genbutsu, and problem solving helps maintain a high level of equipment availability. Planned audits enable management the verification of employees' compliance to existing processes and the closure of any eventual gaps between the process as planned and its implementation. However senior managers' buy off is necessary to make any solution that I listed above work.

A lean enterprise should have green initiatives in order to minimize the use of fossil fuels and fossil material in general. Managers should have recycling programs for plastics, papers, and hazardous materials while protecting the public from contamination. Managers should also look for using green energy power, which in many cases will positively affect their bottom line overtime. As solar energy, bio-fuels, and battery technologies become slightly cheaper, managers of larger and smaller lean enterprises should hire people who may help their enterprises progressively transition toward environmentally sustainable lean enterprises.

5.8.11) Exercises of poor utilization of non human capital resources waste

Group or individual exercise on poor utilization of resources waste 1
A car manufacturer designs a vehicle that is unnecessary too heavy, meaning the weight is beyond customer requirements for static and dynamic strengths. There is waste of natural resources in the form of steel used in vehicles components.

Q1.1) Whom should you involve for resolving this issue?

Q1.2) Draw the process flow chart for designing the vehicle chassis frame assuming that most extra weight is on the frame. Identify waste on the process flow. Hint: Use frame weight specifications: Weight $\geq$ 800 lbs.

Q1.3) How should the specification be changed to minimize weight?

Group or individual exercise on poor utilization of resources waste 2
A Chemical company manufactures detergents loaded in plastic cardboard boxes. The company does not promote recycling of empty boxes to its customers, which leads to fewer consumers recycling their empty boxes. This is waste of material. The waste here does not have immediate negative consequence to the company bottom line.

Q2.1) Give arguments that could convince the executives to recommend that their customers recycle empty boxes.

Q2.2) What would be the consequence overtime if customers do not recycle empty cardboard boxes.

Q2.3) How can the company use innovation to minimize environmental waste. Hint: Cardboard uses wood as raw material and wood is renewable by planting trees. Whom else should the company involve as partners?

Group or individual exercise on poor utilization of resources waste 3

Think about your work. Identify poor utilization of resources waste (human capital resource or non human capital resources) at your place of work. Select one example given by one of your group members.

Q3.1) Describe the poor utilization of resources waste in question
Q3.2) What drove the waste?
Q3.3) Who was involved in solving the issue?
Q3.4) Was reoccurrence prevented?

5.8.12) Case on poor utilization of resource waste

An automobile manufacturer named Great Auto Inc had been growing steadily in the US market until a year ago. While it was growing, it built a manufacturing facility in the Southern U.S.A. For the last nine months, It has seen sales of vehicles that it assembles in the U.S.A decreasing from an average of 9300 vehicles per month to now 6700 vehicles per month. The U.S. plant produces three vehicles, a sedan Sa, which is a very small vehicle of class A and a sedan, Sc which is also a compact vehicle of class C. The third vehicle is a crossover built on the same platform as Sc; it is called Cc. The monthly rate of vehicles Sa has decreased from 3300 per month to 2500 vehicles per month. The rate of vehicle Sc has decreased from 5000 vehicles sold per month to 3000 vehicles sold per month. The rate of vehicle Cc has increased from 1000 vehicles per month to 1200 per month.

The company usually defines its strategies and tactics top down with minimal consideration of the suggestions of employees that execute processes. The senior management team believes that adding a new product will increase capacity utilization. They have a new product already fully designed in Europe. It is a hatchback version of vehicle Sa, it will be vehicle Ha. The senior management team believes because of the urgency, increased sales from Ha and increased advertising will be enough to boost sales to levels that make the company profitable. The U.S. sales team members, the customer service team members, quality engineers, and vehicle engineers are aware of the reasons why sales of vehicles have decreased. They are convinced that it is not a warranty driven quality problem but a problem of customer satisfaction. Customers are dissatisfied of features of the vehicles that do not affect the vehicle basic functions. Two engineering supervisors are now convinced that relying on JD Power data and on the focused group data performed a year ago, a few changes should help boost sales. They contact their manager asking them to contact the head of the U.S operation. Their manager told them that the US operation senior management already had a plan.

Q1) You are the manager of these two engineering supervisors, how will you answer to their request?

Q2) What are the opportunities being missed here? Can you compute the cost of the waste?

Q3) Define the process steps that should help understand the reasons why sales of vehicles have decreased? Hint: start with randomly selected customers and customers that have already given feedbacks on customer dissatisfaction.

Q4) What is the most comprehensive strategy that will turnaround this business in the U.S.?

5.9) Non compliance to organizational codes of conduct waste

5.9.1) Definition
It is the waste realized when employees do not conform to company's code of conduct which includes the standards of ethical behaviors, the law, or the company's working rules and recommended behaviors. The company may gets sued in a court of law, employees may get fired, or the company may lose money, which all lead to waste of financial resources, brand value since the reputation of the organization often diminishes.

5.9.2) Examples non compliance to code of conduct waste
Example s)
 A restaurant manager is stealing cash from the restaurant almost daily.
What is the waste here?

Example b)
A governmental official is responsible for hiring contractors to install a computer network in a major service building. He is looking for vendors that may pay him the highest bribery in cash and accept to keep the side deal unknown. What is the waste here?

Example c)
In a manufacturing facility' a human resources manager promotes only her friends What is the waste? In this case the plant manager finds it out but decides to keep his mouth shut, what is the waste?

5.9.3) Causes of non compliance to code of conduct waste
 When there is a poor communication of a company's code of conduct including ethical standard and expected leadership behaviors then employees do not know the standard of conduct that they need to follow at work. If managers do not lead by examples but breach the codes of conduct themselves then the culture of the organization becomes one that tolerates bad behaviors. In some cases there is a non alignment between the corporate office and regional divisions and non alignment between the corporate office and functional departments such as finance, human resources, manufacturing, or engineering. The disconnect between the corporate office and the divisions will last as long as there no objective audit at each divisions and no removal of political constraints that may help maintain bad habits.

Sometime wrong behaviors become the norm and many employees still remain afraid to speak out because of eventual retaliation. It was the case in the Football International Federations Association (FIFA) of 2015 in which many FIFA's high officials kept on taking briberies of different types to gives their votes to countries looking for organizing a World Cup. In such cases the organization becomes so closed to outsiders that only a whistle blower from a courageous volunteer would break the habits by asking law enforcement official to investigate. The lack of accountability and lack of training are also a cause of non compliance to organizational codes of conduct.

To have people drive accountability the organization has to communicate to them the importance of accountability. Training in the company's code of conduct helps in such a case and support from senior managers is necessary. If senior leaders do not support accountability for non compliance to the organization's codes of conduct through leading by examples, then there will be no change of bad behaviors to better behaviors. Having poor human resources managers who may support their bosses more than they support the organization will also perpetuate non compliance to the organizations' code of conduct.

5.9.4) Consequences of non compliance to organizational code of conduct waste

One of the consequences of non compliance to the organization's code of conduct is the existence of lawsuits against the organization. A lawsuit gives an organization a negative public image and distracts managers and other employees who are involved in the lawsuit. Lawsuits against an organization are costly. Even when the organization wins, it has to pay for attorneys' fees. However when an employee, being a de facto agent of the organization commits acts that arm other employees or the public, the organization has to pay fines that account for millions of dollars and sometimes for billions of dollars. Even when there is no lawsuit, the organization loses in many ways.

Imagine an executive who decides to date a supplier representative. If the board of directors finds the misbehavior out and then fires the executive, the organization loses in time and money invested in hiring the executive and in times and funds invested in having the executive performs a high level job which outcomes impact the current and future bottom line of the organization. Now the organization has to start again by hiring a new executive, investing more funds and time to have the new executive get familiar with current issues and strategic plans that the previous executive was working on. Sometimes except for the breach of code of conduct the executive was doing a good job and it may take time for the new executive to adjust to the same level of work delivery.

Discrimination and the lack of objectivity in the selection and development of employees hurt the organization because the organization misses many opportunities, leading to poor utilization of human capital waste as long as there is no lawsuit involved.

5.9.5) Solutions to non compliance to organization's code of conduct waste

Leaders and managers need to coach and train their employees on non compliance to code of conduct waste and make people accountable when people break either the law or the organization's codes of conduct. When hiring new employees, managers must make sure that the new employees are trained in the code of conduct through certification. Second managers may include expected codes of conduct and expected leadership behaviors in employees' job descriptions and work objectives. Managers must also lead by example all the time even when nobody is watching. They should have the courage to make people accountable by taking the steps that foster behavioral change.

The labor relation department and the human resources department need to have leaders who are impartial, have integrity, and are ready to protect the interests of the organization. Hence, the hiring of human resource employees is critical and their governance needs to include regular audits of human resources personnel in the form of employees' feedback that are anonymous. Anonymity is needed to protect employees who tell the truth about bad behaviors. Auditing other departments is also critical.

The senior leaders set the tone for exemplary behaviors. Senior leaders have the duty to abide to important legal mandates such as the Sarbanes-Oxley Act of 2002 (SOXLEY) which requires executives to follow proper procedure, record, and disclosure of accounting information in order to protect investors of fraudulent activities. All managers and specialists working in finance and accounting must be trained in SOXLEY. Executives and managers must also comply with the Foreign Corrupt Practices Act of 1977 which prohibits executives and managers to make payments to foreign governments in order to close business deals.

When dealing with suppliers and business partners all workers need to avoid conflicts of interest, thus managers must train their employees on policies for accepting gifts from suppliers or business partners. I will not forget the rules of equity. Discrimination and harassment of any sort should be prohibited in organizations and managers need to be sensitive to potential offenses to employees of given social groups when they act or communicate. The human resources department needs to include all the rules that I just discussed above in the organization's code of conduct and other rules such as rules forbidding violence, consumption of drugs so the workplace remains a safe and friendly environment. When communicating codes of conduct, managers need to have in mind that people may not sometime follow rules that they understand.

Managers cannot enforce accountability for misconduct unless they have planned reviews of compliance to the behaviors. Compliance to codes of conduct should be parts of the corporate cycle of improvement using the Deming-Shewhart cycle plan do check act. Managers plan for compliance to behaviors by training and communicating the codes of conduct to all employees. The employees act as they perform their jobs, while managers check using performance reviews and surveys and act by addressing misbehaviors when they exist and by giving improvement plans to employees who have misbehaved.

5.9.6) Exercises on non compliance to code of conduct waste
Group or individual exercises 1

A Pharmaceutical company develops a new drug. To pass governmental regulations it runs many trials but its managers and senior executives decide not to report all the known long-term side effects of one of the chemicals mixed in the drug. The government approves the drug but two years later many patients who use the drug file for a lawsuit because of the side effects that negatively affect their health.

Q1.1) What is the waste here for the pharmaceutical company?

Q1.2) What are the damages to patients and the public?

Q1.3) How can this waste be prevented?

Group or individual exercise 2

A US company decides to enter one African country market. To obtain a business license, the company agent, a US citizen, decides to speed up the process of obtaining the business license and acts like many by offering bribes accounting to $2000 to the business licensing manager (to avoid waiting for up to three months). The manager did not know about the US Foreign Corrupt Practices Act of 1977 which prohibits corruption abroad.

Q2.1) If US officials do not find about this act of corruption, what is the waste for the company? Is there any risk of waste in the future?

Q2.2) What could the waste be if US officials find out about the bribe?

Q2.3) How can this waste be prevented?

9) Summary of Module 1

Without a systemic identification of waste that involves most of the employees, it is hard for an organization to sustain lean enterprise and to evolve into a learning organization. Even the best companies may miss to identify waste such as:

Waste from poor quality driven by production or services

Waste from poor quality driven by product design

Poor utilization of human resources

Poor utilization of non human resources

Waste from non compliance to corporate codes of conduct.

Why? Because waste wrongly appears easy to grasp but in reality there is complexity to it and the notion of value adding activities versus non value adding activities may add up to the complexity without proper training and practice. Another reason is that problem solving is not easy and problem solving starts with the identification and confirmation of problems. Since the scope of problem is often wide as problems of various natures exist throughout the organization, it difficult to significantly eliminate waste without empowering and involving all employees in continuous improvement. This first volume of lean enterprise for business value helps managers, specialists, and other individuals understand why lean enterprise works when employees follow its principles and give the reading a base for understanding wastes in manufacturing, product development, and services.

A reader can master the first module by completing all the exercising and solving the cases individually or preferably in groups. I have defined lean enterprise. I have clarified what lean enterprise is and what is not. I have clarified the notions of value adding activities and non value adding activities with examples from manufacturing, product development, and services. I have emphasized the need to break processes in individual steps and to classify each activity as one among: value adding and necessary activities, value adding but unnecessary activities, non value adding but necessary activities, or non value adding and unnecessary activities.

I have clarified the notion of waste in depth which understanding is a prerequisite for becoming a valuable contributor in the execution of lean enterprise. I have proposed many exercises and cases that make the learning both practical and exploratory. Universities and colleges can use this module for the first two or three weeks of senior undergraduate or a graduate business programs, industrial engineering, or manufacturing engineering programs. The next steps are for the readers to read the next modules of the training manuals which should be available within three months of the release of this first module. The three other modules will be:

Module 2: Reduction of waste in process flow – value stream mapping and other lean tools.

Module 3: Problem Solving and Continuous Improvement.

Module 4: Lean Deployment, two weeks online.

References

Beer, S. (1974). Immanent forms of imminent crisis. *INFOR, 12*(3), 318-330. Retrieved from http://www.utpjournals.com/INFOR-Information-Systems-and-Operational-Research.html

Ford, H. (1926). *Today and tomorrow.* New York, NY: Productivity Press. 1988 edition.

Henderson, B. A., & Larco, J. L. (1999). Lean transformation. Richmond, VA: Oaklea Press

Kennedy, M. (2003). *Product development for the lean enterprise*: Why Toyota system's is four times more productive and how you can implement it. Richmond, VA: Oaklea Press

Liker, J. 92004). *The Toyota Way.* New York, NY: McGraw-Hill

Liker, J. K., & Morgan, J. (2011). Lean product development as a system: A case study of body and stamping development at Ford. Engineering Management Journal, 23(1), 16-28. Retrieved from http://www.asem.org/asemweb-emj.html

Nakajima, S. (1984). Total productive maintenance. Cambridge, MA: Productivity Press

Ohno, T. (1988). *Beyond large-scale production system.* Portland, OR: Productivity Press. Retrieved from http://www.google.com

Qbase (n. d). Shainin's method of practical design of experiments. Retrieved from https://www.google.com/search?client=opera&q=code+of+conducts&sourceid=opera&ie=UTF-8&oe=UTF-8#q=shainin+techniques+pdf

Shah, R., & Ward, P. (2007). Defining and developing measures of lean performances. Journal of Operations Management, 25, 785-805. doi:10.1016/j.jom.2007.01.019

Sharman, S., & Chetiya, A. R.(2009). Simplifying the Six Sigma tool box through the application of the Shainin's DOE techniques. *Vikalpa, 30* (1). Retrieved from http://www.vikalpa.com/pdf/articles/2009/vol-34.1-13-19.pdf

Shingo, S. (1985). *A revolution in manufacturing: the SMED system.* New York, NY: Productivity Press

Sobek II, D., & Smalley, A. (2008). Understanding A3 thinking; a critical component of Toyota PDCA management system. New York, NY: Productivity Press, Taylor and Francis Group. Retrieved from https:boos.google.com

Womack, J. P., Jones, D. T, & Roos, D. (1992). *The Machine that changed the world.* New York, NY: McMillan Publishing Company

Index

Definition of Terms

8D Problem solving: 8D problem solving is a team problem solving method which has eight steps and that requires the formation of a team, the definition of a problem, the definition of containment actions, the identification of root causes, the verification of root causes, the definition of permanent corrective actions, the verification of permanent corrective actions, and the prevention of the reoccurrence of the problems

Autonomation: The control of variations in the workstation where variation occur using automation and human actions. Its synonym in Japanese is Jidoka

Class A surface: It is a plastic surface that has a good appearance, is smooth, usually has needed gloss and even clear coating, and that passengers of a vehicle can see when they enter the vehicle.

Class B surface: It is a plastic surface that has low esthetic and which vehicle occupants should not see when they enter a vehicle.

Gemba: Literally it is the place where the variation or the problem occurs in manufacturing, service, or product development. It means in Japanese "the great place". It is used as a synonym of the Go See process also called Genchi Genbutsu.

Genchi Genbutsu: Genchi Genbutsu is the continuous learning and solving of problems at the source where they happen. Problems generally occur within manufacturing workstations, or where engineers do their works. Genchi Genbutsu means in Japanese "go see at the source".

Go See: Go See is a synonym of Genchi Genbutsu.

Heijunka: Heijunka stands for schedule leveling in manufacturing. It is the planning of production in a way that makes each operator receives the same pattern of workload continuously throughout the shift

Jidoka: The control of variations at the workstation where the variations using automation and human actions

PDCA: An acronym of plan do check act

Plan do check act: It is the Deming-Shewart cycle of improvement which means that when facing a problem to solve, a team has to plan for solving the problem, do the work translated as individual tasks of the plan, then review the progress made on and the outcomes of the tasks, and act through adjustments to the plan.

Poka Yoke: A mistake proofing device or system that prevents one or more specific defects to occur or to exit the workstation

Predictive maintenance: Predictive maintenance is the method for maintaining equipment for which the maintenance technicians look for systems and components that are near breakdown using different testing tools and methods including visual testing, audio testing, tactile testing, infrared thermal analyses, infrared graphical analyses ultrasound analyses fluid analyses, thickness analyses, and other non destructive testing.

Preventive maintenance: The method for maintaining equipment by focusing on prevention, which means the technicians work on the equipment before it breaks down following a planned schedule of standardized tasks using acquired knowledge on the equipment, and causality per statistical methods for maintenance.

Shainin's problem solving: Shainin's problem solving is a problem solving method for which the researchers first look for the factors that explain the variations the most using iterations. Once researchers find the most important factors called in decreasing order red of importance red X, Pink X, and Green X then they find the root causes by determining the ranges of red X that cause the problem observed using inferential statistics (Qbase, n. d; Sharma & Chetiya, 2009).

Six Sigma: Six Sigma is a rigorous team problem solving method that started at Motorola. It has five phases that use statistical and scientific rigor, and other causality tools to find a root cause, and reduce unwanted variations at a level of Six Sigma which account for an unwanted variation rate lower than or equal to 3.4 defects per million. There are two Six Sigma methods, the DMAIC which stands for define measure, improve, analyze, and control, and design for Six Sigma (DFSS) which has many variants..

Total productive maintenance (TPM): Total Productive Maintenance is a maintenance framework which relies on skills development, joined work between skill trades employees and production employees for basic maintenance tasks and continuous improvement in equipment maintainability and availability in order to minimize equipment downtime. Seichi Nakajima of Japan Institute of Maintenance developed TPM at Nippondenso (today Denso Corporation), helped it in Japanese manufacturing companies in 1960s and early 1970s, and later help deploy it worldwide in the 1890s and 1990s (Nakajima, 1984).

Solutions to Value Adding Activity Problems

Solution to Problem 1

Design of a maximum safety (more stable) manual car jack

1. Engineers and sales professionals gather data from customers, current vehicle weights, and currently sold car jacks. Value adding and necessary – Missing the correct customer' requirements will result to waste.

2. Engineers use the data to create design requirements. Value adding and necessary

3. Design engineers, material experts, manufacturing engineers meet to define the initial concept of the jack. Value adding and necessary – there may be waste if wrong decision are made but are not identified

4. Design engineers, material experts, manufacturing engineers meet again to finalize the initial design. Value adding and necessary

5. The team finalizes analytical design verification for fatigue under distributed cycles. Value adding and necessary

6. The design team verifies resistance to static loads using linear and non-linear finite element analyses. Value adding and necessary – value is creating here but minimizing the risk for not satisfying the customer.

7. The design team builds the prototypes in house or outsources the build of prototypes. Value adding and necessary

8. The design team performs functional, static, and dynamic testing using prototypes. Non value adding but necessary

9. The manufacturing team builds production prototype and the design team uses them to adjust the design. Value adding and necessary

10. The design team finalizes drawings and bills of material and the design is ready for production. Value adding and necessary

Solution to Problem 2

A cellular telephone named Star Electronics manufacturer has brought to the market a cellular telephone name Starphone but customers are not buying as many Starphone units. Start Electronic has even thought about discontinuing the telephone but the suppliers and retailers have raised their disagreements. Star Electronics decides to quickly redesign a new telephone called Starphone 2 using feedback from customers and competitor benchmark. Starphone gives itself nine months to bring Starphone 2 to the market.

1. Engineers and sales professionals gather data from customers and competitors' cellular phones. Value adding and necessary – There may be some wastes in derailed steps.

2. Engineers use the data to update design requirements. Value adding and necessary

3. The design team meets to finalize the initial design. Value adding and necessary

4. The design team verifies durability and function using simulation, analytics, and engineering judgment, as well as the initial prototypes. Non value adding but necessary

5. The design team builds second stages prototypes relying on its pilot team and its suppliers and using production tools. Value adding and necessary

6. The design team performs functional, static, and dynamic testing on production prototypes. Non value adding but necessary

7. The design team makes adjustments as needed. Value adding but necessary

8. The manufacturing team builds more production prototypes and the design team uses them to adjust the design and Star electronic proposes them to selected customers for trials. Value adding and necessary

9. The design team finalizes drawings and bills of material. Value adding and necessary

10. The design is ready for production using feedback from the trial. The design is ready for launch Value adding and necessary

Solution to Problem 3

A city office assigns two collectors per shift for each of the five different areas of the city. The collectors work from 7:00 AM to 4:30 PM and cannot go on break simultaneously. The collector's job is to assign a ticket to each vehicle that is wrongly parked or parked too long per assigned city's ordinances. Out of the five collectors, a few starts having behaviors that did comply with the process. Some of them would go on break for too long, which cause them not to cover all the parking spots. Others would give breaks to vehicle owners who should normally receive a ticket at the exchange of a bribe valued at about 25% of the fine. Here, the collectors follow a process that deviates from the prescribed process.

1. Report to work at 7:00 AM in the morning. Non value adding but necessary –

2. Drive a vehicle to parking spots. Non value adding but necessary

3. Identify a vehicle that should receive a ticket. Value adding and necessary – The customer here is the city which represent it inhabitants.

4. Assign a ticket to the vehicle. Value adding and necessary

5. Go on break. Non value adding but necessary

6. Return from break. Non value adding but necessary

7. Repeat steps 3) and 4). Value adding but necessary

8. Report the list of tickets to the city clerk. Value adding and necessary

9. Go home. Non value adding but necessary

10. The owners' of vehicles that receive the ticket pay the fine. Value adding *and* necessary.

11. The city clerk collects the fine. Value adding and necessary